Wales Trails

A bike ride around Wales

ISBN: 978-1537352428

Cover design by Dave Lewis

Photographs by Dave Lewis, Sue Gurman, Eve Phoebe Lewis, Warren Smart, Yago Urrutia and some very kind passers by

Also available as an e-book

For more information contact the author: www.david-lewis.co.uk

Published in the UK by www.publishandprint.co.uk

Special thanks to:
Sue, Eve and Lili for letting me go
Warren and Yago for coming with me some of the way
Warren and Alun for digs and food
Sue and Eve for putting my tent up / support crew
Jeff, Ceri, Dawnne, Merrill, Chris & Noa for 'ride rescue' digs
Mam, Sue, Eve, Alyson, Janine, Babs, Caragh, Greg for welcome
  home party in Llanover Arms
Simon for the book title

Dave Lewis

Wales Trails

A bike ride around Wales

Publish & Print
www.publishandprint.co.uk

For my Dad, who beat prostate cancer

"I
I just took a ride
In a silver machine
And still feeling mean
Do you want to ride
See yourself going by
The other side of the sky
I got a silver machine
It flies
Sideways through time
It's an electric line
To your zodiac sign"

- Robert Calvert

Wales Trails

Background

The last time I decided to cycle anywhere further than the corner shop for a pint of milk and a Tiger loaf was back in 2005 when my friend Derek agreed to go along with my idiotic suggestion that we ride almost 1,000 miles, uphill, from Land's End in Cornwall to John o' Groats in Caithness.

The good news about that trip was that somehow, through much adversity, we did eventually make it. We had a fantastic time, met some wonderful people and got so drunk in John o' Groats that I bet the locals are still wondering what hit them. It was Mark and his awful jokes by the way.

The bad news was that my bottom would never be the same again. Neither would my faith in British engineering, as my brand new Dawes Discovery 701 seemed to have this strange dislike of spokes. Keeping them attached to the wheel that is. So, with the wrong wheels, racers, not tourers, our intricately planned (on the back of a beer mat) historical and wildlife sightseeing trip through England and Scotland quickly turned into a bike shop Trip Advisor adventure!

Ah well, we live and learn. I wouldn't make the same mistake again. Mmm...

When Steve Redgrave said to shoot him if he ever went near a boat again I uttered a similar refrain after pole dancing around the famous John o' Groats signpost back in July 2005. But, after a couple of gallons of Scottish beer I completely forgot about this sacred vow, my tender posterior, seized-up knees, sunburnt hands and aching back.

And like the amnesiac fool that I am I haven't stopped talking about doing a similar ride for the last eleven years. Luckily, no one would listen to me long enough for it to become reality.

A lot can happen in ten or eleven years though. Sadly, my wonderful dad passed away, my mam moved house, and my daughter gave up her bottle, whizzed through primary school, became fluent in Welsh and then metamorphosed into a six-foot teenager.

I started a fabulous new job, teaching computers, digital photography and Photoshop to adult learners about fifteen minutes drive away from the house. Then, about eight years later, I lost it. The job I mean, not my marbles. They went years ago.

Now, as it happens I've always been pretty good at losing jobs. In fact, since 1989 I reckon I must have had over twenty-five or even thirty different jobs, often doing two or three at the same time. Sometimes I just give them up because I get bored or I fancy doing something else other times there are more sinister forces at work. I once gave up a Head of Biology teaching job in a great school with great kids to go to Kenya to look for elephants. A year later, I'd seen the elephants and was back in Wales. Then about a week afterwards I decided to try to learn German and go to the Seychelles to tag turtles. I didn't go in the end. Never been any good at languages.

Usually though I just train others to do my job. That way short-sighted, overpaid managers, who wouldn't know an honest, dedicated and highly-skilled professional if one dropped on their heads from a very high filing cabinet, can shit on me, and somehow, rather perversely, feel good about themselves. 'Ah, love 'em,' I say!

Anyway, I digress. After the epic Land's End to John o' Groats (LEJOG) trip my previous poor health improved, I settled down into normal-ish married life, got the great job, tried to teach my toddler all about the beauty of trees and that there was actually a point to hiking up the three highest mountains in Wales before your seventh birthday, flew around the world and also succeeded in launching my career as a poet back in 2009. But something was missing...

Then, in October 2014, I gave up teaching adults about apertures, shutter speeds and Layer Masks in Photoshop to become a full-time writer. OK, to be slightly

2

more accurate, austerity, local council budget cuts and redundancy money forced me to leave my job, but did at least allow me to pursue my dream.

I signed on for four months but also managed to write a bit and eventually finished, after seven hard years, my fantastic crime thriller trilogy. These were the books that were going to sell millions, catapult me into the literary limelight, see me rub shoulders with James Patterson, Lee Child and Cormac McCarthy, and allow me to live happily ever after sailing my hundred foot yacht around the sun-kissed Caribbean islands accompanied only by my crew of ex-Olympic, Polish, ladies beach volleyball team.

'Oi! Wake up.' My wife Sue was elbowing me. 'Stop watching Dexter and take the recycling out, the ashmen are due tomorrow.'

'OK, I'll do it now, in a minute,' I replied in typical Welsh logic.

'Sue...' a long pause.

'Oh no,' replied my long-suffering wife, knowing what was coming next.

'Can I disappear for two weeks in August?'

'Why?'

'I'm going to cycle around Wales.'

A short pause.

'Yes, OK, paint the decking first though.'

And so it was decided, just like that. There were a few other reasons of course.

Back in 2005 I'd kept a brief diary of our travels and hadn't thought to do anything with it. Then by the end of 2015, it suddenly dawned on me that my previous cycling escapade was ten years ago and that soon I'd be fifty years old! Looking for any excuse not to begin my 'thirty years in the planning, gritty valleys novel', that was giving me real writers block, I thought why not write up the LEJOG road trip? It would give the boys something to laugh at if nothing else. So, paperback and e-book here we come.

I released that book in September 2015 and sold a few copies to my friends and then something remarkable happened. I started to sell half a dozen copies a day on Amazon kindle and was soon propelled up the best selling 'cycling charts' – not exactly Dan Brown or E. L. James but it was a good start! Thinking about it, the 'naughty bits' in my cycling book were probably far more convincing than the 'naughty bits' in the *Fifty Shades* version so maybe that was why it was so appealing? But, the point was, I was suddenly a writer! A professional author. Actually making money from my work. OK, let's get real, only a few quid a week, but even Jesus had to start somewhere with that weird, contradictory collection of self-help books he put together eh! Religion not my strong point either you might have guessed.

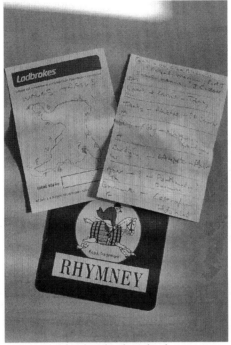

In depth planning!

So, the next step was a spot of planning. Not too much of course, that would ruin the quest if everything went as it was supposed to. Oh, no. Much better to make it up as you went along. An ex-navy friend always told me 'Remember the eight P's – Proper prior planning and preparation prevents piss-poor performance.' Nah, far too Bear 'bloody' Grylls for me, I'll just pump the tyres up and go, how hard can it be, especially in my own back yard as it were. It's not as if I'll be cycling around northern Iraq in a camouflaged jockstrap with a cartoon of some bloke with a beard being friendly to his pet goat on my t-shirt is it?

I'd just buy the latest guide to cycling around Wales and follow that, detouring to bits I knew already to make it more interesting. Easy-peasie. But, that's when I encountered the first problem. I DuckDuckGo'd 'Wales' and 'cycle' books. I found plenty of books on 'parts' of Wales but not a sausage on the whole caboodle. Nothing. Mmm? Very strange. I couldn't find one. Not a single 'around Wales cycling trip' committed to parchment. And so suddenly I had another reason to do the trip. I might have been wrong but no one else seemed to have written an account of a circuit of the Principality since Owain Glyndŵr got chased around the woods by Henry IV in the 1400's.

'Hey, this could be a million-seller,' I told everyone who'd listen. But there was now another reason to do the ride and the book. Although I'd cycled quite a bit around Wales in the past I'd never done a complete circuit and seeing as LEJOG is such an iconic ride for cyclists the world over I thought maybe I could inspire other bikers to start making Wales a 'must-do' ride too. After all we now have the Welsh Coastal Path and so a book that offers any route around my poor, forgotten country could only do good things for the Welsh economy, especially if it encourages other riders to do the same as me. That is, stay at Welsh-owned B&Bs, drink Welsh real ale in Welsh pubs, get my bike repaired in Welsh bike shops, stay at Welsh campsites and eat Welsh cornets at the beautiful Welsh seaside from Welsh ice cream sellers. Yeh, I know, over-doing the patriotism a bit there, but helping to bring cash into the poorest part of the UK can't be a bad thing surely? And think about it, I couldn't do a worse job than the Welsh Tourist Board who only care about golf courses and 5-Star hotels for American or Japanese visitors, so a win-win for the land of dragons and daffodils. Maybe the Welsh Assembly government will knight me or something?

5

Now the first epic bike ride I did, almost 1,000 miles with no training, the now infamous, 'Land's End to John o' Groats, *On a beer mat*', was planned, as the title says, on the back of a beer mat. Well, I wasn't being caught out like that again. No, this time I'd do it properly. Plus I didn't have the reassuring presence of 'Derek the Bike' (no ladies, not like that) to come with me, as he was busy cycling up an alp in Switzerland or something equally death-defying, and so I had to be utterly professional this time. No mistakes. No dodgy wheels with spoke phobias, no cock-ups.

Then, over a couple of pints of real ale in my local I spotted the ideal solution to the difficult, and some might say the most important, planning stage. No beer mat for me this time. So amateur! So last year. Instead I used two slightly damp, Ladbrokes betting slips I found lying around in the 'Wonky' pub, Pontypridd one evening.

That will impress the boys and girls at Sustrans I thought to myself. So, with my borrowed biro (fine confession for a professional writer) safely returned to its rightful owner behind the bar, I had another pint of Rhymney Export and sat back to admire my handiwork, satisfied that this trip was already on a far safer footing then the previous one. Eat your heart out Derek!

Real Planning...

OK, so having scribbled down a rough route around Wales I now needed to check my geography, using Google Maps, and see if it could be done in a fortnight. I say a fortnight because two weeks was all the time my tolerant wife would allow me to be away from home, especially as I hadn't been working for half the year.

The Challenge – to test my fifty-year old prostate gland over a punishing fourteen-day circuit of the Principality clad only in my new *cboardman* gel shorts and a *Life Is Good* 'Happy Hour' t-shirt.

I'd actually designed and printed a special commemorative issue 'Wales Trails' tour t-shirt before I'd even stepped on a pedal so would probably use that one as well. Then I realised just how much work Derek must have done on our last adventure. Shit!

The Route – my plan was to start at the house in Pontypridd, get on my bike, ride through the park, past the University, down to Church Village onto the by-pass cycle route and go behind the hospital, before picking up the Celtic Trail to Swansea. Then hopefully, stay on that until I got to Mumbles, have an ice cream and try to find my mate Warren's house in Three Crosses. The next day was slightly more vague, but essentially I'd use the Celtic Trail again, then detour to Laugharne to see the *'heron priested shores'* of Dylan Thomas's former home before following the coast road to Tenby, where I was hoping to stay with another friend, Alun, who drove up to Scotland with Mark to pick me and Derek up when we did LEJOG all those years ago.

Then the actual route gets a bit flimsy... Celtic Trail again from Tenby to St Davids, same again to Cardigan and then the really tough bit starts. Inland and uphill on the Lôn Teifi route to Aberystwyth via Lampeter and Tregaron, followed the next day by a coastal-ish ride to Barmouth.

Once in *Gogledd* I planned to head for Caernarfon, see the castle, over the Menai Straits to Ynys Môn (Anglesey), do a quick recce around the island before tea and medals at Bangor. Then it was the coastal path and cycle route right across the top of north Wales to Prestatyn, followed by a sketchy plan to find Wrexham. Then I planned on leaving Wales for a bit. Mainly because I'd cycled the length of Wales (Prestatyn to Pontypridd) many years ago with Mark, and also done the Taff Trail about twenty times. So, Oswestry it was then. Here I had a slight problem because I knew nothing about this area of the England / Wales border and just thought it best to follow my nose when I got there. Remember the eight Ps...

I saw a forest on the map so thought I'd head for that 'cos I like trees, get to Knighton, on Offa's Dyke and then head towards the bookshop town of Hay-on-Wye before seeing if there was an easy way around Hay Bluff to Abergavenny. Next, was Chepstow, then on to Newport before trying to see if there was a route worth taking along the coast between Wales' two closest cities rather than do the Caerphilly mountain Celtic Trail I'd cycled years before. Also I couldn't really cycle around Wales and miss the capital city out. Finally, once in Cardiff, I should be OK as it's the Taff Trail north, back to the house in Pontypridd for a few dozen beers in the Llanover Arms and a curry from Mo's to celebrate. Once I'd signed autographs, beaten my way through the media scrum and paparazzi, not to mention the First Minister with his sash and bells or whatever he wears out these days. But all this goes without saying.

Kit – I would use my old Dawes Discovery 701 with proper wheels this time and take two small panniers to carry a few essentials (see full two-week kit list below).

Digs – this was always going to be the biggest expense in 'rip-off' Britain / Wales so I was half-hoping I'd meet some sympathetic, cyclist loving, poet-cum-zoologist with a spare bed and a shed with a big lock. I wasn't holding out too much hope actually. So rather than worry about the cost and any difficulty I might have actually finding somewhere to sleep in the middle of summer in small, quaint seaside towns I did what all men do when faced with a problem of this magnitude – don't worry about it.

Having said this though I did have the first two nights sorted so it was just eleven nights to find as I rode around.

Training – as all professional cyclists will tell you, training is vitally important. So once again I figured high calorie curry and real ale should do the trick. I thought I'd lost weight compared to eleven years ago but the weighing scales in our bathroom seemed to have developed a fault and reckoned I was still 105kg. My knees were still giving me trouble, as was my dodgy chest but the biggest worry I had was my neck. Years of playing rugby had compressed the cervical vertebrae but last summer whilst mountain biking with old college mates Warren and John 'the mad axe man' I somehow managed to catapult myself over the handlebars, through the air, before head-butting a heather-clad gully faster than William Wallace spun a claymore. Four or five visits to the osteopath and an X-Ray from the GP showed my spinal column to be akin to a Cadburys flake – only the crumbliest, flakiest... anyway, the point was I'd have to be careful from now on.

Being eleven years older I figured a few training rides were in order. For LEJOG I did one forty-four mile ride so this time I did double the training! Yep, two thirty-five mile rides, a couple of weeks apart. Yep, that should do it I thought.

You'll never make it,' said Simon.

Yeh, I'll do my training on the way,' I replied, confident that somehow I'd find some hidden strength somewhere.

Transport – for the LEJOG tour we needed to get lifts, as I imagine cyclists from outside Wales, attempting to repeat my ride would do, but for me this was not necessary, as long as my own wheels held out.

Actually for anyone living in Wales, doing the same ride should be quite easy as all you'd need to do is start at one of the points along the route, and then finish there after completing a lap – easy!

For any foreigners coming to the land of fire-breathing women and spit-drenching place names though my advice would be to just get a train to Cardiff, take in a rugby match, February is a good month for this, do the ride (but don't forget the Speedos and vest) and then enjoy a fabulous pub crawl in one of the best cities in Europe. If you want to do the exact route I did though get a train to the city, a valleys line ride to Treforest and stay in a student mate's house.

As for when and what time of year, don't worry about this because contrary to popular belief Wales is actually the sunniest place on the planet outside Fiji, it never rains and the south-westerly prevailing winds just have a calm and soothing effect on the soul. There are no hills whatsoever and the last sabre-toothed tiger roaming the countryside was shot just outside Abercwmboi in 1982. So all good. Who needs Alan Whicker!

Charity – I hoped to cover approximately 500 or 600 miles (never been that wonderful at sums either) and also thought it would be a great idea to raise some money for charity. My joke about prostates, the fact that I was getting near that 'danger age' myself and having a friend working for Prostate Cancer UK seemed to have made the decision for me. A friend from Pontypridd had just been diagnosed, and I'd just designed a website to raise awareness in Wales. My dad had also suffered with the disease many years previous and had, through strength and determination, beaten it. I also figured that on those inevitable moments, when I was cycling against the wind, with my legs and chest burning and was feeling like I couldn't carry on, that this thought would spur me on.

I argued with myself about the choice of charity for a bit (I also wanted to give money to EIA International, the charity that helps combat the endangered animal trade and exposes environmental crime) but eventually decided it would have to be my friend Seren's workplace charity.

I set up a 'Just Giving' page and sent the web link out to a few friends to pass on to their friends and hoped they'd pass it on to their friends and then I'd let viral marketing do its thing.

I sent out (twice) a very professional press release from Prostate Cancer UK to BBC Wales, the Western Mail, SW Argus, Pontypridd Observer, GTFM, Facebook, and Twitter etc. and got absolutely no response from anyone at all – don't you just love the great British media eh! Actually that's not entirely true, the SW Argus asked if I'd be going anywhere near Gwent and the local rag did manage to cut and paste what Sue emailed them. Eventually you just give up with these people though.

Kit List

X1 Bike – Dawes Discovery 701 – great bike, albeit unridden and covered in dust since the last book over eleven years ago, but I did change the tyres and tubes (Gator tyres & Continental tubes) and drip a bit of oil on the chain – what could possibly go wrong?!

X1 Helmet – cheapest Bell model I could find from Halfords (I would have used my old Bell helmet but it split in two pieces when I went over the handle bars of my mountain bike while cycling down Sugar Loaf mountain, near Abergavenny. It saved my life, according to my osteopath and GP, so can't complain)

X3 Spare inner tubes – Halfords (cheaper)

X1 Puncture repair kit (with those impossible to use tyre levers)

X3 pairs of surgical rubber gloves (for oily chain stuff)

X1 small pack of wet-wipes

X1 Multipurpose spanner, set of Allen keys, spoke tightener

X1 Bike lock

X1 small Dual action pump (with small gauge), £15

X1 Pannier rack with two small Arran panniers, £55

X2 Water bottles – to put Lidl's own isotonic pop in

X1 Bike computer – Garmin Edge 200, so when I finished I could look at the hill profiles and realise what a crazy idea it had been

X1 Cycling top (well, actually it was a walking, base layer from Trespass but it did the job)

X1 T-shirt with 'Wales Trails' logo (for when too hot for cycling top and also in case I had to prove I was cycling for charity when begging lifts or digs for the night)

X2 *cboardman* gel cycling shorts (£10 cheaper online than in Halfords store, so always ask them to price match after you try them on)

X2 Pairs walking socks – Gellert ('cos I like to buy Welsh when I can)

X1 Karrimor walking shoes – yep, the same old pair I wore on LEJOG and still in one piece (just)

X1 Waterproof (well, not really) coat – from Mountain Warehouse (why pay three times as much for a different brand and a more expensively designed logo?)
X1 Cycling gloves – Aldi (fingerless, from Crane)
X1 Sealskin gloves (long-fingered, spare pair in case it got cold in the Hinterland)
X3 Pants – one on, one off, one for beers in the night
X2 T-shirts – for pub in night (took two just in case someone recognised me wearing the same one twice)

My kit for the two weeks!

X1 Cargo shorts (Saltrock)
X1 Sandals – old Merrell pair (to air the feet after spending nearly two weeks sweating in eleven year old daps)
X1 Small compact, waterproof, shockproof, digital camera – Canon Powershot D30 – more than adequate for taking basic snaps of the beautiful Welsh countryside (battery, charger, SD card)

X1 iPhone 5 (off EBay). I even ditched my old PAYG tariff of approx. £20-£30 a year and started an expensive £5 a month contract. I wanted to be able to use the Google Maps and Internet if I ever got lost. Did I say *ever*? The really great thing for me about modern phones though is that you can put hundreds of your favourite music tracks on them. I tried to use a different song for each early morning alarm. I suppose I could have used the phone camera to cut down on weight but call me old fashioned I like a real camera. One drawback with an iPhone though is that although it has lots of apps and gadgety things it doesn't appear to have one of those things for getting stones out of horse's hoofs? I hope those boffins down at Apple take that on board and I look forward to the next battery-draining version

X1 'Curry card' (i.e. Lloyds bank Visa / cashpoint card) – for B&Bs, campsites, cycle repairs, buying prawn or tuna sandwiches, Turkish Delight and Red Bull in Spars, not to mention the pig-out evening meal or chippy visit washed down with some first class real ale that has to be the highlight of any cycling trip in the UK

X1 Print outs of various maps (Celtic Trail and Lôn Teifi only, as I figured the North would be easy enough to find and coming back I was going to use mostly minor roads anyway)

X1 Diary / pen – so I could write about all the great people and places I encountered on the trip, and also to send all the boys a postcard describing the great time I was having without them, especially as they'd promised faithfully to come with me but at the last minute needed to wash their hair…

X2 Plastic bags – to put pants and t-shirts in when it rained (this is Wales remember)

X1 Shower gel (small) – to keep the weight down

X1 Toothpaste (small) / brush – ditto

X1 Sun cream F30 (small) – in Wales, lol, ditto

X1 Toilet roll – in case I got caught short near a castle, coracle or a cathedral and had to make a hasty retreat to the bushes

Pontypridd (the day before the off)
Thursday 28th July 2016

iPhone alarm: The Sensual World – Kate Bush

Had a lazy day around the house. Packed the panniers and watched some awesome Stereophonics videos on YouTube. Got worried I'd forgotten something, had a panic attack then took the dog for a walk. Then I logged on to Facebook to learn that my cousin had passed away in the night. He'd been bravely fighting throat cancer for over two years and it suddenly put my little bike ride into perspective.

I went to 5 a side football as usual at 5:30pm and tried not to get injured. Managed to survive an hour of running about and afterwards in the changing room I listened in silence to Aled and Simon telling me separate stories about friends of theirs that had recently had crashes on their bikes.

One chap had died and another was in a coma, unlikely to recover.

'Ta boys, just what I needed to hear before I set off.'

'Just trying to cheer you up mate,' said Simon.

Went home, had a nice cooked dinner (my last for two weeks) and a couple of beers. Then Warren texts to say he's stuck in work and can't make it. He might turn up tomorrow...

 Day 1

Pontypridd to Three Crosses
Friday 29th July 2016

iPhone alarm: Destination Anywhere – The Commitments

Wake in darkness with a bad back and a stabbing pain in my groin. My arthritic foot is agony from last night's football. It's raining.

I doze until 6:45am, then open my eyes to my wife, Sue, doing yoga while Lili the Labradoodle jumps on the bed and licks my ear.

Outside the Llanover Arms in Pontypridd

Over breakfast Sue reminds me it's been over eleven years since I tried anything like this.

'Thanks for that,' I say.

Then at 8:00am there is a knock on the door and it's Warren, with a bike in his car boot.

Last minute preparations over (another cuppa) we set off at 8:30am, down to the Llanover Arms, Pontypridd (my local pub) for a *start* photo. Then it starts to rain again, right on cue, as we push off and head to Ynysangharad War Memorial Park and the Taff Trail.

We whizz through the park, and pass the triple-arched Machine Bridge, the world's oldest stone railway bridge, which was built by the industrialist Dr Richard Griffiths to carry horse-drawn drams of coal from the Rhondda valleys to join the Glamorganshire Canal at Treforest in 1809.

Warren next to the monument

We quickly leave Treforest and the local 'Degrees R Us' University by taking a left off the pavement and onto the old railway line that runs alongside Llantwit Road. A great little trail where you pass huge stone walls and a rusty metal outline of Tom Jones, the Treforest born singer whose sold over 100 million records yet never put a penny back into his hometown.

A couple of miles later and we're on the Church Village by-pass cycle trail that eventually connects us to Route 4 – the Celtic Trail heading west. We shelter under trees at the shopping centre before pedalling down past the Royal Glamorgan Hospital and emerging like drowned rats at the burger van. Warren decides to sample the £2 meaty sandwich, which he nearly throws up because it's so bad, while I chat to a local dog walker.

We stop for a moment at the old Coedely colliery site and I remember I'm supposed to be taking photos of this trip. Warren is impressed by the way they've reused the old machinery to build a monument. Looks like they ran out of money (or ideas) for a lake or park though on the old site.

During the peak coal mining period of the 19th Century Coedely Colliery employed nearly 1,800 men, which changed the face of Tonyrefail and the surrounding area forever. We continue to Thomastown and the rain eventually eases. We miss Tonyrefail, which is a shame because I could have mentioned that King Edward II was captured by forces loyal to Queen Isabella near there in 1326.

A steep hill to Tynewydd and then rough gravel lanes downhill past wind turbines and lots of open fields all the way to Blackmill. Next up we wind through some lovely lanes and purpose built bike trails to Tondu, another old coal mining village servicing the Parc Slip Colliery. It's about here we bump into Santiago (Yago), a Spanish cyclist on his way to Ireland via Fishguard. We have a quick chat before he speeds off.

On the 26 August 1892, a huge explosion shook the Parc Slip Colliery, over a hundred men and boys died with just thirty-nine survivors. Some remained trapped underground for a week before being rescued. Sixty women were widowed and twice as many children left fatherless. The mine closed in 1904. Now there are no jobs here but a beautiful park. I think I prefer it this way.

We cycle through a small forest and then the Parc Slip Nature Reserve where I slip, slide and skid off my bike and onto my knees as we negotiate some wet decking / boardwalk. Warren is too busy laughing to take a photo though. Yago is just up ahead and we have another quick catch up before he cycles off again.

Pressing on past Pyle we take a detour through Margam Country Park, an estate of approximately 850 acres. It is situated about two miles from Port Talbot. It was once owned by the Mansel Talbot family. Within the park are three notable buildings, Margam Abbey, a Cistercian monastery built in 1147, Margam Castle, a neo-Gothic country house and the 18th Century Orangery. No one offers us any half-time fruit though.

Trying to get in to Margam Park with our bikes

When I say we go via Margam Park though we only just manage it due to the bloody ludicrous gates that seem to be some sort of Krypton Factor puzzle! Warren manages to use his engineering background to solve the problem though and we thread our bikes and kit into the crystal maze.

Of course, as a zoologist the best bit about the park for me is the *Cervidae*. The deer herd dates from Norman times although some say they were here during Roman occupation.

Originally just Fallow deer, in the last fifteen years firstly Red deer and then Pere David deer have been introduced and thrive in the park. The Pere David are an endangered species and in the park they are part of a breeding programme in conjunction with Whipsnade Safari Park.

We cycle on rough gravel tracks, not really suitable for road bikes and catch up with Yago again. As he leaves us once again I say to Warren, 'You know what's going to happen don't you?' He takes his phone out and rings Nicola, in Gower, 'Hi Nic, set another place for dinner, just in case will you.'

We speed out of the park and head for the beach. Well, actually we head for Port Talbot, because it's in the way of the beach.

Steelworks, Port Talbot

The earliest evidence of humans in the area appears to be from Bronze Age farming ditches around 4,000 BC. There were Iron Age hill forts scattered all around too. Modern Port Talbot (if you can call it modern) is a town formed from the merging of multiple villages, including Baglan and Margam, and centred on Aberafan on the west side of the river Afan. Port Talbot first appears in

1837 as the name of the new docks built on the east side of the river by the rich Talbot family.

The town is famous for the steelworks and the constant cloud of smoky air pollution that hits drivers on the M4 as they pass. We weren't so lucky and had to cycle through the streets of the town while ingesting some sulphur-smelling gas – lovely!

Chips at Aberafan beach

Port Talbot does lay claim to many famous people though, for example, Sir Anthony Hopkins, of Silence of the Lambs fame, was born and raised here. Just up the road in the pretty little village of Pontrhydyfen, where there is another great cycle trail, a certain Richard Jenkins was born. He moved to Port Talbot where he met his mentor, Philip Burton, and changed his name to Richard Burton.

Allan Martin, with the toe-poke kick, one of the stars of the great Welsh sides of the seventies, played for Aberafan and the rugby posts have wizards on top.

Dic Penderyn, was born as Richard Lewis in Aberafan in 1803. He was convicted of assault on an army soldier and executed.

We arrived at 2:30pm and headed for the chippy. Parking the bikes on Aberafan beach for a bite to eat in what can only be described as a bracing summer breeze.

After a tray of carbohydrates and some sausage sandwiches with pickle for lunch we cross Briton Ferry bridge and the River Neath before heading towards one of Wales' biggest employers – Amazon. Then we pass the new University buildings that look like something out of *1984* on Fabian Way.

The city of Swansea is thought to have developed as a Viking trading post, although there is evidence of people living here from the Stone Age, Bronze Age and Iron Age. The Romans also visited but didn't stay long.

Swansea is Wales' second largest city after Cardiff with a population of 462,000 (in 2011). During its 19th Century industrial heyday, Swansea was a key centre of the copper industry, earning the nickname 'Copperopolis'.

Trendy Swansea Marina

Like Port Talbot the city has many famous people, most notably the poet Dylan Thomas who called the city an 'ugly lovely town'. Other celebrities include the singer Harry Secombe, actress Catherine Zeta-Jones and musician Spencer Davis.

On the sporting front Swansea stars include Nicole Cooke (cyclist), John Charles (footballer), Mervyn Davies and Shane Williams (rugby union).

We hit the marina and the posh developments at the front and Warren suggests a small refreshment seeing as we're in spitting distance of his house on the Gower. We stop at a trendy café, sit outside and I buy two pints of crappy Italian lager for £9. Remind me never to volunteer quite so quickly again!

'Make sure you enjoy every mouthful of that beer,' I tell Warren, when I relay the price with a grin.

'Oops,' he replies.

'It's cheaper in Copenhagen!' I continue...

Just then a bike whizzes past and we catch glimpse of an orange cycling top we've not seen for a while. It's Yago! On his way to find a campsite down the Gower somewhere no doubt.

Warren quickly jumps on his bike and races after him. Eventually I see the two of them heading back to the bar where Yago buys himself a beer and joins us.

'So, where are you staying?' asks Warren.

'Well, I haven't found anywhere yet,' says Yago.

'OK, I'll phone Nicola again. Tell her to put an extra pizza in the oven.'

Swansea Bay

Beers downed (we didn't take the glasses back) we saddle up again and head for the sea. We pedal along the front of Swansea Bay with the sandy beach to our left and the start of the Mumbles to our right. Past the White Rose pub (where many years back Warren famously abandoned his car, ran away from the local constabulary, did a smash and grab for a bottle of whisky and ended up on a train to Swindon) and instead of heading up the hill we continue to the lighthouse and pier.

Not sure why I wanted to add on extra miles to a long hard day but guess it was nostalgia. Many years ago we used to get a minibus from Cardiff University, down to Mumbles, to do the 'mile'. There used to be about twenty pubs there and we often tried to have a pint in each one before staggering into 'Cinders' for a dance. OK, I never actually danced, call it a wobble. Don't think we ever managed the lot, although I do recall one time in college when we managed four pubs and got banned from three. I blame Brian and Cheyne.

Mumbles Pier

In fact, in later years, and slightly older and wiser, we used to have minibuses from the valleys down to Mumbles too. Don't think I ever managed the whole route then either.

Can't remember all the pubs' names but I think there was the White Rose, The Nags Head, CJ's, Vincent's,

William Hancock, Social Club, Rugby Club, Monroe's, Prince of Wales, Antelope, Conservative Club, Nab Rock, George, Pilot, Yacht Club, Toby, Salty bar, Cinderella's, Admiral Benbow and Neptune's.

What I do remember is us students doing 'selfies' with an old film camera (invented circa 1985-1989), climbing over the rocks to get somewhere dangerous at 4:00am and laughing so much in the chip shop we wet ourselves. Ah, happy days.

Boys at Mumbles

Nowadays you'd be lucky to get half-cut if you just had a pint in each pub as most of them are shut. Such a shame and a sad reflection on our healthy lifestyles, beers at home, the demise of pub culture, lightweight students, camera phones linked to social media and the inflated prices breweries charge for just water and yeast really. Got to Mumbles, skipped a Joe's ice cream and took Yago to see the pier and the lighthouse at the end of the line.

After leaving the pier we head back along the front and cut inland towards Clyne Park. A nice uphill trail through the trees until we somehow stumble upon a lovely country pub. I don't know how you do it Warren?

A nice pint of real ale at The Railway, Upper Killay is enjoyed at the beer garden at the back of the pub, right on the bike trail. Then we head for the road and up a big hill, across the Gower and soon we're in Three Crosses. Nicola greets Yago in a language we guess is super-fast Spanish. Quite easy for her as she is a Spanish and Portuguese teacher, as well as being examiner for Wales.

Lighthouse, Mumbles

Yago is well impressed anyway. We have a quick catch up, nice hot shower in Warren's new bathroom (very nice mate) and then some great food (pizza X3, tuna salad, some funny, foreign-sounding things that I hadn't had before and can't remember the name of, plus beer and red wine).

Then I suddenly realise I'm aching like never before, even after all that training, and maybe fifty years old wasn't the perfect time of life to embark on a round Wales cycle trip.

We think about a visit to the local pub but then realise it's not a good idea with an even longer day ahead tomorrow and hit the sack, or in my case the purple room, which is now brown. Don't ask, it's a woman thing and only they can ever know the answer to that question, which is best not asked in the first place.

The Railway

Cycling Stats

Start: 8:30am
Distance: 59.02 miles
Total Distance: 59.02 miles
Average Speed: 9.24mph
Fastest Speed: 24.59mph
Cycling Time: 6 hrs 23 mins
Finish: 7:00pm
Calories: 3404
Ascent: 3900 ft
Descent: 3743 ft
Beers: 3

Route

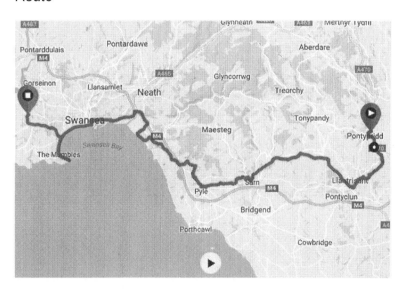

Hill Profile

 Day 2

Three Crosses to Tenby
Saturday 30th July 2016

iPhone alarm: A Mi Manera – Gipsy Kings

Wake up 5:00am ish, couldn't sleep, mainly due to pain in both knees, bad back and stabbing pain in groin. Doze until my Yago-dedicated alarm call goes off and get up by 7:00am.

Garden version of BT telephone box

Nice day in the Gower. Nicola has already left with son Wills, who wants to win Wimbledon one day, so he plays a lot of bat and ball stuff. Warren makes tea and does

29

porridge and bananas for us all. Now we're talking! Proper athlete fuel.

'Rub a dub dub, here comes my grub!'

Warren arsing about with his bike for ages, doing stuff like pumping tyres, oiling chain, checking his kit, all that unnecessary fussing that cyclists like Derek do. Eventually leave at 8:45am, a bit late for my liking, knowing how far was ahead.

Downhill through the village of Three Crosses and find Route 4 again at the bottom of the hill, where Warren points out a BT phone box. Another relic of the past, now that everyone uses mobile phones. It's in good condition to be fair with not too many stingy nettles or brambles growing inside, although the door has seen better days and whether you'd actually get a dial tone or be able to force your 10p in the slot I don't know?

Great coastal path cycling, Loughor

Anyway, enough about telecommunications, onwards the three musketeers pedal and through the lanes we soon reach the pretty little village of Loughor.

There's a nice old castle there, established by Roman soldiers from the Second Augustan Legion in about AD 75, to guard their communications route that crisscrossed south Wales and included the River Loughor, but we had bigger ruins to chase and headed for the Loughor bridge.

We rode along the Millennium cycle path, really nice route, very flat. Came to Llanelli (North Dock) where I simply had to try and tackle a stationary Phil Bennett. Unfortunately for me the old British Lion has still got it. I could only watch in awe as he promptly handed me off and swiftly sidestepped through the gap whilst wrong-footing All Black Kirkpatrick.

Lions legend Phil Bennett

Anyway, onwards we went, along a great trail until a few yards later. 'Bang!' Yep, my first puncture. Start counting now... For those that remember (or have read the previous cycling book) on the last epic cycling trip I embarked upon (LEJOG, 2005) readers were encouraged to count the bike shops we visited due to the crappy spokes I had. This time the maths will be confined to tallying up inner tubes.

Yago wastes no time in jumping to my rescue and quickly whips off the super-stiff Gator skins and inspects the inside of the wheel for sharp pointy things. He then checks the tape before stuffing a new inner tube in (glad I brought three), pumps the tyre up and off we go again. (See Derek, who said I had to learn how to fix a puncture?)

This is probably a good time to recap on the wheel situation of my Dawes bike. When I bought it online over eleven years ago they supplied it with the wrong wheels but after numerous nasty emails from me they very kindly sent me two replacement wheels (with more spokes) free of charge. I sold the old racing wheels to Aled and fitted my new £120 each wheels to the old bike. So, I figured (incorrectly as it happened) that all my troubles were over. I had tidy wheels; they'd cope with my sixteen stone mass of blubber plus panniers weighed down with Mars bars and bottles of Lucozade. I changed the tubes and bought new super-tough tyres. What more could I do? Mmm, don't answer that.

Me, Yago and Phil

All patched up we think no more of what appears to be just a minor freak accident and pedal on west. We pass loads of new builds; holiday homes and lets that have a strange, deserted, lifeless Orwellian feel again, must be a Swansea builders thing?

We reach Burry Port harbour, a small town five miles outside Llanelli in Carmarthenshire. The town is famous because Amelia Earhart landed here as the first woman to fly across the Atlantic Ocean. Pilot Wilmer Stultz actually flew the plane and Amelia was just a passenger when they left Newfoundland in 1928 and landed at Pwll near Burry Port, exactly 20 hours and 40 minutes later, but why let the truth get in the way of a good story eh? There is even a commemorative blue plaque at the quay.

Kidwelly Castle

We cycle on through the Pembrey Burrows sand dune and wetland system until we reach Kidwelly, and then head up to the castle for some lunch. The original castle was built in 1106 by the Normans and is quite famous because in the 13th Century Edward I 'Longshanks' included it in his strategic 'Ring of Iron' oppression against the Welsh.

A field nearby is known as the location of a battle in 1136, in which Princess Gwenllian led her husband's troops into battle against a Norman army during his absence. She is believed to have been killed either during the battle or beheaded at the castle shortly afterwards.

Either way the two day old sausage and pickle sandwiches were still going strong and thanks to Warren we supplemented the meal with Welsh cakes bought from the local shop and washed it all down with Lidl's own Lucozade – I bet Bradley Wiggins never ate this classy!

After dinner we push on to Ferryside and take a quick look at where the old ferry used to cross as well as admire the stunning views across the water to Llansteffan and it's castle. I love Llansteffan and cry with joy whenever I read (or should that be re-read) Dylan Thomas's *Visit to Grandpa's* – one of my favourites. The image of Dai Thomas in his best waistcoat is one of the best descriptions I've ever read saying what it is to be Welsh.

Llansteffan Castle, from Ferryside

We head out of Ferryside and before we can have a crack at a nice hill... yep, you've guessed it – puncture number two, oh dear. It starts to rain.

Yago and Warren are not impressed, so we start the clock and see how fast we can change the tube. Well, actually, Yago takes control again and decides that the tear in the tube is in the same place as last time so we think it might be the wheel. We check for protruding bits of metal again, find a likely suspect but it's so small, dismiss it.

This time though, instead of swapping tubes we stick a plaster over the hole and pump it back up. It seems to hold and we figure an extra layer of rubber might save it if it is indeed the inside of the wheel rim.

We cycle up and down what seem like a million hills (probably wasn't quite that many) until we reach Carmarthen, one of the oldest towns in Wales. It was certainly around when Ptolemy was putting ink-filled marsh grass to parchment or whatever they did back then. A Roman fort is believed to date from around AD 75.

Some say Merlin was born in a cave outside the town but I never heard anyone from Savannah's nightclub confirm this. We crossed the bridge over the Towy and looked for a bike shop. Eventually found it using Google Maps (I had my iPhone upside down – oops), but it was closed, bugger.

Warren resting just before the tractor panic!

I thought Yago was leaving us at Carmarthen and heading across country to Fishguard but when I suggested we say goodbye he looked kinda sad. My bloody Alzheimer's playing up again. Last night I told him he could stay at Tenby with us in Alun's flat and he'd agreed to delay his Irish ferry by a day or two. I forgot.

'Sorry buttie, I forgot,' I said.

'It's OK,' Yago smiled back.

So onwards we went, me continually ill at ease riding over any bump, thinking my tyres would explode or deflate any second. Most disconcerting.

We found a load of lanes (still Route 4), looked for shortcuts but it was a waste of time really. We just accepted the pain of uphill, downhill, and then repeat!

We looped to St Clears, asked directions in a pub but didn't stop for a pint (serious stuff now) and on we went. Found a lovely trail by the river but decided to skip Laugharne, the writing shed, castle and ice cream van as I knew there was a big hill out of there and because we'd wasted so much time on punctures. Been a million times anyway and we were running late, although I would suggest other riders do visit if you haven't before. Well worth it for the *'pale rain over the dwindling harbour, and over the sea wet church'*, and you can easily see how Dylan got his inspiration.

Yago fascinated by *Boa taurus*

Further on, at the top of a hill, we rest for a moment for Yago to take a photo of some cows that took his fancy when half a dozen silage tractors and trailers inch past each other, going up on the grass verges opposite to squeeze through the narrow road.

My bike is left haphazard on the tarmac and I'm across the road taking a photo of Yago and his Holstein Friesians. Warren is peeing himself at the thought of my Dawes getting squished to a flat cowpat shape! The drivers must have seen my 'Wales Trails' t-shirt though and took pity on us.

We push on and after a big uphill know that we have a great downhill into Amroth to look forward to as reward. It is indeed a great downhill and Warren and Yago enjoyed every yard of it, unfortunately for me with half a mile to go I round a bend, see the glorious beach ahead and I hear a loud bang followed by a hiss and a wobble of the front wheel.

I won't repeat what I said. Still counting folks? Yes, it's the third puncture in a day.

It's a long walk down to the beachfront and the pub. Amroth is famous for having a petrified forest under the sea (visible at low-tide), destroyed when sea levels rose 7,000 years ago, with fossilised antlers, nuts, animal bones and Neolithic flints. I just know it as Eddie and Nicola's place though, 'cos a former teaching colleague owns half of it now.

New Inn, Amroth

I was going to suggest the Smugglers but Warren had already got a round of ice-cold lager in the New Inn. He also ordered chips all round as I cursed and kicked my doomed bike while Yago wondered why these Welshmen were so hot-tempered compared to the far calmer Spanish temperament.

I gulped down what was probably the best beer in the world at that point. Then we fix the puncture, which we're now becoming quite proficient at to be honest.

Suitably refreshed by a second pint of lager we decide it best if we at least try to get to Tenby before darkness hits us.

Amroth beach

We cycle along one of the most popular and beautiful coastlines in Wales. Go through tunnels with just a few hills and reach Saundersfoot where although the summer light over the sea is stunning the majority of residents just seem to be stocking up on 24-packs ready for the weekend. The Welsh love to do things in excess eh! Not that me or Warren would know anything about that of course, always the first two tucked up in bed with the cocoa us.

Saundersfoot is an old medieval Welsh town and grew in size after the harbour was built. The Saundersfoot Railway and Harbour Company began to export anthracite coal, in 1829, from the many mines in the area, although coal was exported from the beach for centuries before this. The village grew up to serve the port, which by 1837 had five jetties handling coal and iron ore and subsequently pig iron and firebricks.

The town is now a typical seaside resort with its famous New Years Day swim attracting thousands of crazy people. We stop for a moment to take in the sights and sounds of Saundersfoot before heading up the big hill out of town, past the Gower Hotel, that used to be privately owned by a lovely guy called Steve who me and Sue used to know. He used to have a speedboat that he'd take us out in. Now, unfortunately the hotel is owned and run by some awful, impersonal chain.

Yago, Saundersfoot

It's a big drag up the hills but we're determined to reach Tenby, the jewel of West Wales. I just made that up. Tenby (Welsh: Dinbych-y-pysgod, meaning fortlet of the fish) is a walled seaside town in Pembrokeshire with colourful houses and awesome beaches.

The picture postcard town, especially the view from above North beach must be one of the most photographed (and Photoshop'd) images in Wales, if not the UK. I have a few myself. This wonderful 13th Century medieval town now only has the Five Arches barbican gatehouse left of the original walls, plus a few ruins scattered amongst the place.

The town's property prices are certainly not medieval though, unless you're thinking torture. The English immigrants, mostly from the rich south east, have inflated prices so high that few local people can afford a one-bedroom flat in their hometown.

How times change. In 1650, a plague epidemic killed half the town's population. By the end of the 18th Century the town was abandoned by the merchants, and slid into ruin. Younger locals probably hanker for a return of *Rattus rattus* to get themselves on the property ladder.

Me and Warren, Tenby

Nowadays there are more than two hundred listed buildings in and around Tenby. In the summer the place is rammed with tourists from all over the UK and on weekends it's also full of stag and hen parties. Many's the time I've just been about to order a pint of local Tenby Harbour pale ale when I've been struck in the face by a giant, pink, inflatable penis.

Boats sail from Tenby's harbour to Caldey Island, where a small group of monks live, but if you do visit remember girls are not allowed. Just like some of the pubs actually, who won't allow hen parties in.

If you want to become a monk it's quite easy though. You just need to be a Catholic, unmarried and not in a relationship, fit and in good mental and physical health, with no debts or dependants, with a reasonably well balanced personality, generous, intelligent, with a sense of humour, and (usually) under fifty years old. I think that counts me out on just about everything!

We admire the view on North beach, Yago takes some photos and we cruise through town, down to the railway bridge, across the road to the Co-op and stock up on carbohydrates. I rummage around for Alun's key and one last hill and we're hauling the bikes and panniers up two flights of stairs to the flat, which will be home for the night.

We were lucky to have a place to stay of course and Tenby, as you would expect, is quite expensive to find digs in the summer. Although it's Saturday night in party town we decide to eat in, Yago cooks a lovely Spanish pasta dish (no idea what was in it but it tasted lovely), we have a couple of lagers and a bottle of red wine to wash it all down with.

I text Alun to get some logistical information – like where is the hot water switch, then curse him for not replying to my texts and start to shiver in my sweaty *cboardman* shorts and t-shirt. I forgot he's on holiday with the kids in Corfu.

Tea finished we look for our best trousers to hit the town with. Well, actually we don't. We just look at each other through half-closed eyes, know it's a really bad idea, stick Monty Python on the telly (the one with the bespectacled, West Country Mr Pither and the cycling trip to Russia – what else!) and laugh ourselves to sleep after a gruelling twelve-hour day.

Cycling Stats

Start: 8:45am
Distance: 66.41 miles
Total Distance: 125.43 miles
Average Speed: 9.51mph
Fastest Speed: 32.58mph
Cycling Time: 6 hrs 58 mins
Finish: 9:00pm
Calories: 4378
Ascent: 4856 ft
Descent: 5229 ft
Beers: 3
Wine: 2

Route

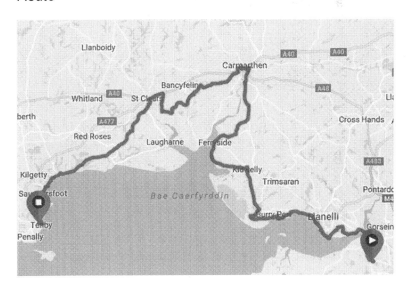

Hill Profile

 # Day 3

Tenby to St Davids
Sunday 31st July 2016

iPhone alarm: Blue Sunday – Tom Petty

Up by 7:00am, quick pack, cup of tea, tidy the flat (Alun's a stickler for doing the dishes) and into Tenby town for some breakie.

Stunning Tenby

We try The Fat Seagull for a full Welsh breakfast with freshly squeezed orange juice and are pleasantly surprised to be served by a Cardiff lass and a bloke from Treherbert. Great food, £3.99 for scram (OJ and tea on top).

Warren decides my portly frame resembles a fat seagull so forces me to have my photograph taken. Then it's back in the saddle (yep, before you ask, I'm sore) and through the arches and down to South beach to show Yago the view of one of Wales' other best beaches. We just have so many.

Sixteen stone plus breakfast

We head off down the hill and soon see a familiar Route 4 signpost. We take the trail through Kiln Park, dodging impatient, early morning drivers in a supposedly 5mph limit caravan park and pass the giant limestone kiln complex that gives the park its name. The Limestone was sourced from the adjacent Blackrock Quarries and coal was brought in by boat from Saundersfoot. The kilns made quicklime or Calcium Oxide. The site closed in 1902.

Limestone, quicklime and slaked lime are used to neutralise excess acidity e.g. acid rain in lakes and soils. Limestone is also used in building, to purify iron in blast furnaces, for making glass and cement so is quite important. Nowadays we import more and more though.

We crossed the roads and headed for the lanes and cycled past Penally, where there's a nice deserted beach. Up and down a few decent hills until we reach The Ridgeway, then carry on. Wheels going well so far, so I'm happy again. Big hill out of Lamphey, heading towards Freshwater East.

'Hey Warren, isn't Pembroke the other way?'

'Yeh, we'll see a sign soon, I'm sure.'

'Does Freshwater East one mile count?' I ask.

'Shit.'

'Stop! Stop! Wrong way Yago!'

Yago turns around and comes back to two Welsh lads frantically checking their Google Maps.

'Oops.'

Confidently heading the wrong way!

We cycle back to Lamphey. The good news is the hill we killed ourselves cycling *up* has now become a *down*. We whizz into the village and see the sign does indeed point south (to Freshwater East).

'Shouldn't that be pointing north or west,' I ask.

Warren grabs hold of the signpost and turns it around the right way.

'Bloody kids, lol.'

And there be the lesson folks, never rely on Sustrans to tighten screws. On we go to Pembroke.

We make it to Pembroke, the birthplace of Henry Tudor (Henry VII), the first monarch of the House of Tudor just in time for some tea. He ruled the Principality of Wales until 29 November 1489 and was also Lord of Ireland.

Henry won the English throne as well when his forces defeated King Richard III at the Battle of Bosworth Field, the conclusion of the Wars of the Roses. Henry was the last king of England to win his throne on the battlefield.

Henry needed a quick victory as Richard had reinforcements in Nottingham and Leicester. Though outnumbered, Henry's Lancastrian forces decisively defeated Richard's Yorkist army on 22 August 1485. Richard III was killed while searching for a 'horsey' according to Black Adder and Shakespeare of course.

Pembroke Castle, birthplace of Henry Tudor

We decide to stop for a look around and end up doing a lap of the town looking for a beer garden. Eventually we settle for an indoors café, get some hot coffee, toast and jam, served by an English owner who seems intent on selling us everything his poor, struggling hotel business can produce. Carrot cake, Victorian sponge, full English breakfast, snacks, more cakes, various types of coffee I've never heard of and so on.

I give him a card and explain we're doing a charity cycle ride for Prostate Cancer.

'I've got some more cake out the back if you want,' is his reply.

We take a few minutes to admire the splendid Pembroke Castle. Originally built in 1093 by Roger of Montgomery during the Norman invasion of Wales, it was given to William Marshal by Richard the Lionheart a century later and rebuilt in stone creating most of what remains today.

The town itself though dates back much further, mainly due to the natural harbour that offers shelter from the elements. There is evidence that people, including the Vikings, used the Milford Haven estuary for many thousands of years prior to the Norman Invasion in 1066.

We jump back on the bikes and cycle around the water at the back of the castle. The sun is shining and it's a beautiful day. Just perfect for a slow puncture. Yeh, looks like my back tyre is going down a bit. About 40 or 50psi instead of 100 is the estimate we all agree on.

We wind through lanes, lose the Route 4 signs for a bit before threading our way down through the houses of Pembroke Dock to find the Cleddau Bridge over the estuary.

The first bridge collapsed in 1970 but the 1975 version seems to have been designed better. There is a toll for cars but we just waved ourselves through like royalty and got hit in the face by a ferocious cold wind. We stopped to admire the view and the camera appeared again.

The views are magnificent, both up and down the Cleddau estuary and after reaching dry land again we soon find some great traffic-free lanes all the way to Haverfordwest. A really nice section of undulating, well-designed bike trails.

Warren had been getting regular updates on his father-in-law (who was rushed to hospital yesterday) and decided it was time to get the train back to Swansea. Yago also needed to leave us and get a midnight train to

Fishguard. There he would connect with the ferry to Ireland to continue his journey to Galway.

View from the Cleddau Bridge

While the lads cycled to the train station to check timetables I used my mobile's map to locate a Halfords (always handy on a Sunday). Had a great wheel service from Scott, who trued my spokes and suggested I invest in some fabulous slime-filled inner tubes that would immediately seal if I ever got a puncture again.

I bought three tubes (buy two get one free offer), Scott swapped one over for me free of charge and with the wheel fiddling it came to £29. A complete rip-off but one I was glad to pay (at the time) if only to give me peace of mind as the slow puncture was really starting to get me down by now.

Incidentally, have you ever noticed how every salesman you ever speak to these days has got one of whatever product you happen to have in your hand at any given moment? Apparently Scott, and the other guy there always used these fantastic inner tubes and they cycled around the world most weekends. I've noticed this phenomenon quite a lot in Halfords actually.

'Yeh, I have some of these myself, they are awesome!' says the salesman.

So you buy them and a week later they turn out to be a complete pile of shit.

Anyway, enough of that, I'm sure he was trying his best. I cycled out, convinced my wheel problems were over and whom should I bump into outside Sainsbury's but Yago.

I popped inside bought him a large granary loaf and a bar of Turkish Delight. No idea why, guess I'm just a hopeless romantic. Although he did say he wanted something for sandwiches.

I relayed the latest wheel / inner tube saga and we hugged in true Mediterranean style, wished each other well and I cycled off into the sunset like John Wayne. Actually I didn't leave him there, Sainsbury's is no such place for that, I showed him the town of Haverfordwest, the river, and the shops and then I left.

The town is a weird one though, English-speaking for centuries, south Pembrokeshire is known as 'Little England Beyond Wales'. Maybe this is why Christian Bale, who was born in Haverfordwest, doesn't like to be reminded of the fact. 'Hey Christian, you're Welsh!' Other famous people associated with the town include actor Rhys Ifans of Twin Town fame, and Chelsea Manning, the sex change US soldier who leaked tens of thousands of US Military documents. Told you it was a weird place!

Back in the saddle I cycled a few miles back out of Haverfordwest to the trails again and looked for Route 4 signs. I found some pointing up some hills – great news.

Warren texted later to say he'd had to catch the train to Swansea with his bike. He was meeting Nicola at the station, who passed him his car keys through the window, before he cycled the Taff Trail from Cardiff up to Pontypridd to retrieve his car!

I head towards Broad Haven, manage a couple of big hills before I stop for my sandwich and Lucozade. Sat by the side of the road on this deserted country lane I could be anywhere. The silence is wonderful, apart from the gentle breeze and the occasional burst of bird song – it kind of sums up the loneliness of the long distance cyclist.

A bike, some panniers stuffed with calories (and inner tubes in my case), some water and isotonic drinks.

With the boys gone it's easy to let the mind wander and I wonder if I'll ever make it without moral support. It's a long way around Wales and I'm only on day three. My knees are killing me, my shoulders and neck ache, my bike is playing up and I've still got a fair few miles to go to get to St Davids, the cathedral city the size of a large village.

Broad Haven

The carbohydrates kick in and I'm off again. Suitably refreshed I remember I'm rolling on super-duper inner tubes and gator tyres. My confidence soars as the glucose hits my arteries and I'm off again, up and down through some long lanes heading towards the beach on a glorious sunny afternoon. I start to descend, pick up speed, I see the sea. The light on the water is enchanting. I hit almost thirty miles an hour coming into the town and I've made it. I stop for the last of my food, attempt to take a selfie while eating, not my best look, and look forward to the campsite that Sue has just texted to say she and Eve have found.

Off I go again, along the front and up a big hill out of Broad Haven. I push myself to get to the top as I know I have bigger hills to come. I look forward to seeing Solva again, home of the Welsh Bob Dylan, Meic Stevens.

I'm in high spirits now as the weather starts to resemble August, my bike is finally going great and I have only fifteen miles to go to St Davids where I'll meet up with the family.

I go up and down some mega hills and then guess what. Yeh, correct. Puncture number four, this time the front wheel again.

Strangely enough I don't panic. The back tyre has a new slime-filled tube (to deal with the slow puncture) and now this front one will have a new tube too. I calmly sit down on the grass next to a small bridge in Nolton Haven and do the necessaries. I pump up the tube to 80psi, all good so far. I take some more sugar via the last of my Lucozade and off I go again.

I climb up a huge hill and then down into the start of Newgale beach. I like Newgale. This is real rugged Wales. Fantastic coastal scenery with the path winding up and down the cliffs.

Had enough now!

Newgale is one of over forty Welsh 'Blue Flag' beaches, which means it has the top certification for quality and cleanliness. There is a large pebble wall or storm beach as defence against the high tides and the bracing winds are perfect for windsurfers, surfers and canoeists.

I'm seven or eight miles away from my support crew at St Davids. 'Bang!' 'Phhhiiiiissssssss'.

This time it's the back tube. Green slime oozes out of the wheel, covering my gator skins and making them look like Pete Venkman in Ghostbusters! This is puncture number five. I text Derek, who is half way up a Swiss alp, on his way to his holiday home, log cabin on the Baltic. He suggested I buy gator skin tyres.

My earlier elation is soon replaced by despair. Nothing for it now. I phone Sue for a lift. I sit on the grass and wonder if my safari is over. I try to weigh up my options. Should I just drive home and come back with my mountain bike tomorrow? Should I drive home and get the bike repaired, preferably with new wheels? Should I just buy a new hybrid bike with tougher tyres?

As I'm sitting there a man sits down on a bench nearby.

'Puncture is it?' he asks.

I felt like punching him in the face for stating the bleedin' obvious but instead smiled back.

'Yeh, it's my fifth one in two days. My wheels are knackered I reckon.'

'Might be the rough roads?'

'No, it's the wheels mate.'

'Might be you're too heavy, especially with all that weight in those saddle bags?'

Fist clenching now…

'Aye, might be.'

'I've been touring around Wales for years. I promised myself that when I retired I'd go to every little cove in Wales. I bought a camper van.'

I couldn't give a shit mate!

'That's nice,' I reply.

'You'll get cold sat there.'

No shit Robert Boyle!

'Yeh, it's getting chilly now.'

'You should take the bike to Cardigan, great bike shop there.'

'Pardon?'

Why is he suddenly making sense?

'I'm from Knighton. Been touring around here for years though.'

'What bike shop?'

'Yeh, one of the best around so I'm told.'

'In town is it?'

'Aye, I think so. Met lots of bikers on my travels, they swear by it.'

I could kiss him! Well maybe not, he's got a beard.

Twenty minutes has turned into forty minutes before I realise Sue is lost. I dig my iPhone out of the zip pocket. Ah, no charge, that's helpful. It doesn't even last a day when you use Google Maps! How many billions of dollars profit did Apple make last year and they can't even invent a decent battery! Probably got shares in energy companies.

An hour passes, I'm shivering with cold and then I see the familiar sight of Scooby Doo flowers on a black Kia. I put the useless pile of British engineering on the roof rack and drive to the Duke of Edinburgh pub for chicken burger, chips and beans with a much-needed lager that didn't touch the sides.

Then we drive to St Davids, then out to the campsite. I take a long hot shower, drink a bottle of Corona lager and finish Eve's leftover strawberry cheesecake for supper in the tent. I recharge the phone and surf the Internet trying to see what bike I could buy if the bike shop turns out to be Halfords (i.e. crap).

Support crew at campsite

Have a logical think about the future of the trip and decide it would be a nightmare to use my mountain bike as it would be too slow for the number of miles I want to do. I could buy a new bike but that would be way too expensive, I'd probably need £500 plus for a half decent replacement, and it might need building, tweaking etc. So for *Plan A* I plump for repair the Dawes!

I fall asleep dreaming of green slime oozing out of my brain.

Cycling Stats

Start: 7:00am
Distance: 44.03 miles
Total Distance: 169.46 miles
Average Speed: 9.11mph
Fastest Speed: 28.19mph
Cycling Time: 4 hrs 50 mins
Finish: 7:30pm
Calories: 2997
Ascent: 4157 ft
Descent: 4124 ft
Beers: 2

Route

Hill profile

 Day 4

St Davids to Cardigan
Monday 1st August 2016

iPhone alarm: Thunder Road – Bruce Springsteen

Slept a couple of hours, dreaming of blowouts, slippery rubber and lots of sweaty pumping. Make your own mind up.

Up by 6:00am, pack my stuff and take down the tent with daughter Eve still inside. Send a quick text to my friend Dawnne, who is away with another mate Davis, camping somewhere. She replies with her sister Merrill's number.

A great shame I missed cycling through St Davids, which is the resting place of the patron saint of Wales and the most overpriced accommodation in the Principality. It's actually more expensive to stay here than in Cardiff, which is just crazy.

Back in the day, Dai and his brothers kept bees and fed the poor. In the 6th Century he founded a monastery here. The original cathedral was burnt down and destroyed by Vikings. Always party-poopers those damn Vikings.

The present cathedral was built by the Normans and contained many relics, including the remains of St David. Many pilgrims, many of who were nobles and kings, including William the Conqueror in 1077, Henry II in 1171, and Edward I visited it.

Pope Calixtus II decreed that two pilgrimages to St Davids were equivalent to one to Rome. A bit like two visits to the Llanover Arms in Pontypridd are equivalent to one to the Old Arcade in Cardiff.

Over the years the town became a city because it had a cathedral, then lost it's status 'cos that wasn't good enough anymore, then got it back after someone sent a letter to Liz, the queenie. But I digress, I missed the smallest city in the UK because I was on a mission from God. Unlike Elwood though I had to get a bike together!

We drove to Fishguard with the bike sat on top of the jeep. Through town, then down to Lower town. Don't worry, it's a Welsh thing. The bike seems happy to see the sights without my sixteen stone plonked on top of it. I take a photo to prove my bike made it to Fishguard. Well I had to show willing, I was riding for charity after all.

Fishguard dates between 950 and 1000 AD and was probably a Viking trading post while Lower Fishguard grew up as a herring fishery and port.

In 1779, the port was raided by the privateer Black Prince (of Llantrisant nightclub fame) who bombarded the town when the payment of a £1,000 ransom was refused. As a result, Fishguard Fort was completed in 1781.

The Royal Oak pub was the site of the signing of surrender after the Battle of Fishguard in 1797, the last successful invasion of Britain, when a force of 1,400

French soldiers landed near Fishguard but surrendered two days later. The story is told in the Fishguard Tapestry created for the 200th anniversary to emulate the Bayeux Tapestry, and is displayed in the Town Hall Library.

The Dawes sightseeing

Lower Fishguard was used as 'Llareggub' in the film of Dylan Thomas's Under Milk Wood, starring Richard Burton, Elizabeth Taylor and Peter O'Toole. Many local people were involved in the production of this film as background characters. In fact 'Rich' stood two gardens down from Sue's great auntie's house for the famous film promotion shot.

Next, we drive to Cardigan and decide I need some fat as well as carbohydrates so we head for the best café in the whole world. The Rendezvous café in the market, run by champion rower Jan, and her friend Emma. Jan is actually the daughter of a world famous Coracle maker / fisherman and when we explain our predicament she gives us a big discount on the food, plus an extra pot of tea for free.

Then it's time to take the Dawes Discovery 701 to the bike shop. It's like going to the dentist. Fingers crossed.

Eve and I are staring through the window at the bikes, wheels and other cycling paraphernalia when we see the opening hours sign. Shit! An hour to wait.

Then it starts to drizzle. We're just about to walk away when a man appears on a motorised bicycle. I have a good feeling about him.

'Hello, are you opening up?' I ask.

'Yeh, you're early, give me a minute to switch the alarms off.'

We enter New Image Bikes, Cardigan and I have verbal diarrhoea.

'My bike's broke.'

'I need two new wheels.'

'Can you do it now?'

'I mean, if you have them in stock, if you have time.'

'Anything tidy, I have to get back on the road tomorrow.'

'It's a charity ride see.'

'For Prostate Cancer UK.'

'You can have my old wheels as a tip, do what you want with them.'

'They're £120 each!'

'Can you fix it?'

Luckily, the man's name wasn't Jim, but Tom. Tom Wells, former Maths teacher and now the greatest mechanic in the world after my Uncle Will.

National hero Tom does indeed save the day (and the entire expedition) by looking at my bike, shaking his head a few times, making that long drawn out whistley sound that builders, garage owners and other tradesmen (who have you over a barrel) usually make.

I'm joking, he didn't. He just cracked on, first thing Monday morning too! Tom fitted two new wheels, a 32mm back wheel, a 28mm front wheel, followed by tape, tubes and tyres, new brake pads (was going to get around to that sometime honest), and we noticed I'd snapped the pannier rack so I bought a new one of those too.

Inflated the tyres to 100psi (front), 80psi (rear) and did a quick ride around the block in the rain to test the new kit and a last tweak of the derailleur mechanism and bill time.

'Oh dear, how much?'

'£210.43,' says Tom.

'Bargain!'

'Glad you think so,' adds Tom.

'And please keep the Dawes wheels and gator skins as a tip.'

'Are you sure?'

'Yeh, glad to be rid of them, psychologically I'd feel better, really.'

And so it was back to the café to tell our new best friend Jan the good news. Then me, Sue and Eve drove off to Aldi (or Lidl, I can never remember), got a few beers and some wine as house-warming pressies and off to phone Merrill.

I like Cardigan. It's a proper west Wales town and still retains a lot of the old charm that many seaside towns have lost. It lies on the River Teifi and marks the border between Ceredigion and Pembrokeshire.

The town dates from the 11th Century when the Normans built a castle here and was the location of the first National Eisteddfod in 1176. Contestants came from all over Wales, England, Scotland and Ireland to compete for chairs in music and poetry. In 1227 a weekly market was established which, incredibly, continues to this day. Although what's on offer has changed quite a bit.

In recent times Cardigan grew as a substantial port. In 1815 it had over 300 ships. This was seven times as many vessels as Cardiff. It also had a thriving shipbuilding industry, with many being built in St Dogmaels, to which we were now heading (bike proudly restored on the roof rack).

Another interesting fact about Cardigan was that in the mid 19th Century there were more than sixty pubs in the town. Unfortunately though nothing lasts forever (not even sex with me) and with the coming of the railway in 1886 the port declined.

One cool thing that does endure though is the Welsh language, with 70% speaking God's language. Now if the local council could help bring the pubs back we'd have heaven on earth.

Spoke to Merrill on the mobile who directed us to the house in St Dogmaels. Raining quite bad now, but as I keep saying, it is August, it is Wales and global warming isn't happening is it Mr Trump?

'Hi Merrill, great to meet you, although I must say you look familiar.'

'Probably seen you around Ponty sometime,' replies Merrill.

Then the conversation goes a bit André Breton.

St Dogmaels

'Aye, I used to play rugby with your dad, Jeff, for Cilfynydd, weird thing was I bumped into him, in town, last week when I brought my canoe up from Tenby to paddle from Aberporth to Llangrannog to look for dolphins.'

'Yeh, he said something.'

'Mind you, I said don't worry we've got a caravan to stay that night, then it turned out Elaine's daughter who was getting married had her hen do that weekend.'

'So then I rang my mate Davis to ask for Dawnne's number...'

'Ah Davis? That's probably where we've seen you. Did you go to Winchester for the wedding?'

'Yeh! Did you see Chuck Prophet too?'

'Yeh, awesome gig, especially getting them up on stage to sing them a song.'

'I know, I was in tears. So was Karen when she came off stage, she was picking glass out of her feet.'

'We stayed in some weird place just out of town.'

'So did we... with Bod and Bev.'

'Who?'

'I bet we were in the same place, fancy that.'

Merrill & family

Introduced to Chris and Noa and had a good chat about all things *Ponty*, rugby, cycling and beer (what else is there in life?). Sorted panniers (my daily routine now) and then babysat Charlie the beagle puppy while the gang went to see the *BFG* in town.

Everyone came back early though as the cinema was fully booked so we had a shower and got ready for some beers. We went to the local pub, via the riverside walk. It was still raining quite heavy but I had a nice chicken, chips and peas washed down by just the one pint of lager. I decided to limit my alcohol intake because I knew tomorrow was going to be really tough. I'd planned it to be the longest day's ride of the whole trip, over seventy miles.

I was also a bit nervous about my *Six Million Dollar* bike – the bastard Dawes.

Oops, that should read the bastardised Dawes.

We had a good night out with the gang but as much as I wanted to drink beer until it came out of my ears it was early to bed for me (by 10:30pm) as I planned to be off by 6:00am in the morning. I set my iPhone alarm and hoped I'd be well and truly back on the road again by choosing a favourite Bob Dylan track from his seminal 1975 album Blood on the Tracks.

The Telegraph has described the song as *'The most dazzling lyric ever written, an abstract narrative of relationships told in an amorphous blend of first and third person, rolling past, present and future together, spilling out in tripping cadences and audacious internal rhymes, ripe with sharply turned images and observations and filled with a painfully desperate longing.'*

Aye, that's exactly what I thought as I fell asleep.

Cycling Stats

Start: 6:00am
Cycling Time: 0 hrs 5 mins
Time in bike shop: 4 hrs 0 mins
Finish: 10:30pm
Cost: £210
Beers: 2

 Day 5

Cardigan to Aberystwyth
Tuesday 2nd August 2016

iPhone alarm: Tangled up in Blue – Bob Dylan

Up by 6:00am, top up the water bottles, a quick cup of tea, two chocolate pastry things and some orange juice then a quick play with Charlie the beagle and I was ready for the off. Looked at the BBC weather report on the iPhone app and it was basically rain all day with strong winds coming in later on – great! Perfect cycling weather, not. It did rain (of sorts) for 70-80% of the day so not too bad I guess, although the winds were saving themselves up for the day after. Right Behnaz Akhgar you owe me an ice cream from *Joes* for this!

Drizzle in Cardigan

Sue dropped me off at town (every mile counts) as I needed to find the Route 4 signposts. I did this and was just about to ride through Cardigan town centre in the rain

65

when I thought I'd double-check with a guy working on the ash cart.

'No, not that way, Newcastle Emlyn is back that way,' he advised.

Cardigan Bridge

Mmm? Confused before I start now. I checked the Google Maps and sodden print outs I had from a Sustrans book. It said back the way I'd just come? OK, back over the bridge and then all became crystal clear, through the heavy, grey drizzle, there was a cycle route along the riverbank.

Got very wet and sweaty in minutes even though it was a nice gentle section to begin the day. I didn't want to think good thoughts regarding the bike as it was early days but it was going well so far. Even the brakes worked in the rain.

Cardigan is in the county of Ceredigion, which has been inhabited since prehistoric times. There are hundreds of hill forts and standing stones dating back to the Bronze Age in the county and many pilgrims passed through Ceredigion on their way to St Davids.

I knew I had a long day ahead so I thought I'd push the pace a bit, seeing as I had some nice flat lanes. Soon got to Cennarth Falls (where the Timotei advert had been

66

filmed). All I saw though were three local fishermen who were after some sea trout. No blondes, no tits, nothing. I don't believe it, just my luck!

I did see the touristy tearooms and some pubs (all closed at this ungodly hour). And on the wall of The White Hart was a cool coracle. The coracle is a small, roundish boat traditionally used in Wales (although similar boats have been observed in Ireland, India, Vietnam and Tibet) and has been in use for centuries. They were even around when Julius Caesar invaded Britain in the first century BC and possibly even during the Bronze Age.

Cennarth Falls

I stop for a few photos then cycle on across the bridge and up a big hill. Then after a mile I realise I'm going the wrong way, head back and see I missed the sign for the trail as I crossed the bridge.

Back at the bridge I go up a hill and soon wish I hadn't. It's a hell of a steep hill. I manage to get to the top and then wind my way, up and down as the drizzle soaks me through to the bone. Such a pleasant pastime this cycling lark.

I reach the bottom of a nice downhill and see the sign for Newcastle Emlyn, which used to have one of the highest concentrations of pubs anywhere, but alas those glory days have long gone. The ruined 13th Century castle was seized by Llywelyn the Great during the revolt of 1287-88 and also by Owain Glyndŵr in 1403.

Rain, rain and rain

The nearby village of Adpar is famous because in 1718 Isaac Carter established the first printing press in Wales there. Then I turn up the mother of all hills and head into the wilderness. Well, it seemed like it at the time anyway.

Lots of ups and downs again, loads of wildlife about, birds and rabbits everywhere, then I make it to the Teifi Valley Railway. It looks cute, like a little *Ivor the Engine* type place so I shelter from the elements for a bit, take a quick look around the very small gift shop, try to say hello to the not-very-friendly woman working there before jumping back on the bike.

Next up is the village of Llandysul, famous these days for wool, canoeing and The Welsh Harp Centre, where the traditional Welsh instruments are made. I stop at a café for a bottle of Fanta. I almost don't because not one of the six people behind the counter can be bothered to serve me but just before I leave the drink there on the bar and walk out a young girl decides she does want my money after all.

I sit in the window and am initially ignored by the two blokes either side of me. I put it down to my smell, which must have put them off their breakfast to be honest, but then one chap does eventually speak. He's English, much friendlier than the locals I've met so far and we have a good moan about the weather in true British-style. He then tells me about a huge hill to Lampeter. I sigh.

'So which way are you heading?' he asks.

'Yep, I'm going that way,' I tell him.

I leave the café, which is next door to an estate agent called 'Dave Lewis', which is a bit weird. I pop in and give the lady behind the desk a business card. She smiles and my faith is restored in the local populace.

I go downhill out of town, around a one-way system, along some quiet lanes, then up through a forest. I stop near the top of a big climb and start to walk for a bit. I'm feeling cold again and the rain seems to have set in for the day.

I'm sweating with my waterproof on so I undo the zip. Then the cold drizzle starts to chill my bones again and I'm suddenly feeling very low. For the first time I start to have doubts. I wonder what the hell I'm doing. I'm fifty years of age and could be at home now, tucked up in a warm bed or better still a warm pub.

69

I'm tired and feel lacklustre. I recognise the signs. I need glucose. I'm on top of a deserted farm track feeling very blue when suddenly I sense something on the wind. I'm not alone. I look up and hovering just ten or fifteen feet above my head is a huge red kite – utterly beautiful, I smile to myself and my spirits lift. I take out my iPhone and write:

> *grey tarmac, grey sky*
> *cold damp hopeless heart*
> *- Red Kite rescue*

I watch the magnificent creature for a few minutes as he swoops over the drenched fields and then he's gone. I jump back on, pedal to the top of the hill and can see rolling lanes ahead. I grab an energy bar from my pannier, take a big chunk and on I go. There are some more big climbs but eventually I reach a T-junction and a long downhill brings me into Lampeter town centre.

Lampeter has a long history but in recent times it was the town that William Edward Julian Cayo-Evans marched his Free Welsh Army from in 1968. Educated at posh English school Millfield (the same as Gareth Edwards) he saw active service fighting communists in Malaya.

He seems to have been radicalised during the building of the Tryweryn reservoir (that Meic Stevens sings about). He was convicted of conspiracy to cause explosions in 1969 and sentenced to fifteen months imprisonment.

In 2000, the Tomos Watkin brewery renamed the Apollo Hotel in Cardiff to The Cayo Arms. The pub is still a regular haunt for Welsh nationalists today, especially the rich media types from BBC Wales, because the extortionate prices are bound to put more working class people off.

I meet up with Sue and Eve, who've driven on from St Dogmaels this morning, on their way to find a B&B in Aberystwyth. We sit in a café where I visit the toilets with a clean pair of pants and cycling shorts tucked under my arm. Suitably refreshed I join Sue and Eve for a huge bag of chips and a pie.

'Wow, that's better I say,' handing Eve my soggy underwear in full view of the lunchtime customers.

'Urgghh!' says Eve.

'David!' says my wife.

'Jesus Christ dad!' adds Eve.

'What? Mmm, nice chips.'

'OMG,' says Eve.

'Now I know what colonic irrigation is all about,' I say, stuffing yet more greasy calories into my mouth.

'What's he like?'

Outside I replenish my Lidl, isotonic drink stocks from the jeep and use the cardboard that came with the pack of four bottles to improvise a rear mudguard for the Dawes.

'Should have thought of this before.'

'Well, you don't expect rain in August do you?' laughed Eve.

Looking very happy (but not gay)

I say goodbye to the girls and head off. My mood is much better with a warm, fat stomach and a clean, dry botty to cycle on. What more could a man want? Don't answer that.

I cycle for a few miles through more lanes and make good time. Then I notice something really weird. A lot of the fields around here have pink sheep in them! I think no more of it until I come upon a sign, just outside a small Welsh village made famous by *Little Britain*.

No, the farmers must be taking the mick? OK, they weren't all pink, more purple, or lilac I suppose. Ah well, each to his own I say to myself.

I had a quick look around but apart from the nice church of St David, which dates from the 12th Century, on a 7th Century site, Llanddewi Brefi only offers drizzle, so I cycled on.

Talbot Hotel

I headed for the famous town of Tregaron, which got a royal charter in 1292 from Edward I. It was here that I met Viv Davies, on his way home with some fish and chips. He wanders up to me and starts to speak.

'Something in Cymraeg I didn't understand.'

'I'm cycling through Wales, heading for Aberystwyth,' I replied, hoping he hadn't asked me if my hovercraft was full of eels.

'Ah, OK bach, doing it for any charity?' asks Viv.

'Aye, Prostate Cancer UK.'

'Good man,' he digs in his pocket for change but only has £2 in coins.

'Have this and put down Viv Davies, Tregaron RFC.'

'Ta buttie.'

We chat for a while outside the famous 13th Century Talbot Hotel, that has an elephant buried in its garden. Viv tells me about the Red Kite re-introduction programme and points out where the farms that helped were.

We soon discover we have a mutual friend, who used to teach PE in my daughter's school.

'Aye, he gave it all up to go off and do something else.'

'Aye, some Christian sect or something wasn't it?' I say, subtlety never my strong point.

Viv laughs.

We chat about the teaching profession (we're both ex-teachers) and how soul-destroying it's become. I think to myself, Wales is a cool place. Here I am cycling through the rainy gloom in the middle of the Welsh hinterland and I bump into a bloke who plays rugby, used to teach PE and shares similar views to me. The words 'small' and 'world' are used again.

Viv seemed like a great character, as you'd expect him to be, coming from the small drovers town of Tregaron, and I'd wished we'd had longer to chat. I say this because there was a long line of characters that'd come from the town in the past.

Recently, in the 18th Century, it was home to *Plant Mat*. A local innkeeper, Matthew Evans had two sons and a daughter who were famous outlaws that hid in a cave near Devil's Bridge. After several years of mayhem they were eventually executed for murder. Sounds like the BBC TV series *Y Gwyll*.

73

And of course these weren't the only outlaws associated with the town as every Welshmen's favourite hero, Twm Sion Cati, was also born here around 1530. Often wrongly termed the 'Welsh Robin Hood', Twm was a protestant at the time of queen Bloody Mary I, who loved killing anyone who wasn't a Catholic, a bit like ISIS who also kill anyone who doesn't agree with them. How times have changed eh?

After a spell as a farmer Twm had no real choice but to take up banditry as a means of survival. His numerous adventures saw him outwit many outlaws and highwaymen.

Wildlife Reserve

As a youngster he fled to Geneva in 1557 to escape the law but when protestant Queen Elizabeth I came to power he was pardoned and returned to Wales two years later. He was a learned man though, he wrote poetry and ended up as a magistrate and mayor of Brecon. There is a wooden statue dedicated to him in Tregaron.

When I was ten years old, and on a rugby tour to Llandovery, I remember me, 'Froggie' and 'Dougie' found his cave on Dinas Hill, Rhandirmwyn. Happy days.

Viv then directs me to the trail, just past the wildfowl centre and off I pedal again. I soon turn off and rest up to take in some glucose, via a sandwich and a sugary drink.

The track is rough and stony, the wind picks up quite a bit and I decide it's best to push on. I'm a little worried about my tyres on the gravel but they serve me well – thanks to Tom from Cardigan. I think about a detour to Strata Florida but decide against it as I'm doing well clocking up the miles on my longest day.

Then, suddenly the mist descends and I'm alone on the barren mountain. A chill begins to spread over my clammy body. I stop for a moment to finish a chewy bar and stick some more calories in. The wind starts to howl all around me and I start to feel a little scared. What if it gets dark? I'll never navigate my way through this wilderness. What am I thinking? I've got hours yet, it's summer after all. Then I see her! Just up ahead. Standing there, statue still.

The ghostly figure then begins to walk slowly towards me. I make out the round, neatly trimmed, dark hair. She stops, right in front of me. She's staring. Staring straight at me. I stare back. She stares harder this time, her blue eyes look straight through me. It's cold and damp on this moorland but she makes no effort to do up the zip on her red parka.

She continues to stare at me. I carry on staring back. She looks at me, I look at her. It's like a scene from The Good, the Bad and the Ugly. I want to speak but something stops me. Maybe it's the lack of a decent script? Maybe I'm dreaming?

Yep, I am. Well, daydreaming anyway. Mali Harries is nowhere to be seen, or her bloody red coat. Shame, she's quite a babe as it happens, but no, she's gone.

I get back on my bike and start pedalling towards Aberystwyth on the Ystwyth Trail. I pass under an old railway bridge near Ystrad Meurig, then through one of those really annoying gates that Sustrans put in the most awkward of places. I cycle along an overgrown path. I see the stingy nettles too late, I fall off swearing like a trooper. I couldn't possibly repeat what I'm screaming to no one in particular.

I dust myself down and push through the greenery, a bramble cuts my thigh.

'Oh hello,' I say, to the young mam with her two young kids climbing a gate to avoid the vegetation I'd just fallen into.

'Hello,' she replies.

We chat for a bit about the trail and the likelihood of more poisonous plants. She assures me there are no more and it's a great ride all the way to Aberystwyth.

Ystwyth Trail

I carry on and find a great downhill near Trawscoed then carry on until I find the river. This great trail follows the river all the way into town and is very much like the Taff Trail, back home in Pontypridd. Mostly flat, with a few handy downhills thrown in for good measure as I quickly clock up more miles on my way down to sea level.

The trail gets quite muddy in parts but thanks to my improvised Lidl cardboard mudguard (sheer class this guy!) my bottom is only 98% covered in wet rain and dirt. I cruise along the trail, check the mileage, know I'm getting closer and then suddenly out of the woods darts a great spotted woodpecker – one of my favourite birds and another timely mood lifter.

There are a couple of hills as you get near to Aberystwyth but nothing serious. I finally reach the beach and think I've made it but I'm south of the town by a couple of miles. No problem, I push on and eventually reach the old college, the dilapidated pier (full of drunk Brummies) and then the ancient town itself.

Made it!

I ring Sue and Eve, who've managed to find a nice B&B just two doors down from me. I was supposed to be booked in to Lwynygog Guest House (£25 a single, no breakie) but as with most things *booking.com* related this isn't what happens. I'm actually staying in a shitty student let across the road. No worries though, just need a hot shower and somewhere to store my now awesome bike. There isn't anywhere, so I carry it up the stairs and it gets a better night's sleep than me.

It's great to ride into town, rather than push a bike with green slime oozing out of deflated tyres, as has been my experience so far! Praise again for Tom, off to the room, clean some of the mud off the bike, pack, unpack, repack, shower and shave, phone Mam, then out on the lash!

There is evidence of Mesolithic hunter-gatherers near Aberystwyth (that's about 10,000 years BC) and some parts of the town still look like they're still here. The Bronze Age inhabitants built a fort overlooking the town around 700 BC but that still didn't stop the English coming. I'm joking mun!

The middle ages saw Gilbert Richard (known as Strongbow) build a fortress here in 1109 but that was replaced by, yes you've guessed it, that crazy castle builder Edward I's effort in 1277.

Welsh hero Owain Glyndŵr lived in the castle between the years 1404 and 1408 but lost it to Prince Harry (the future King Henry V of England, not the bloke with ginger hair that used to dress like Hitler).

Sue & Eve

We went out for something to eat and it was here in The White Horse pub that I realised my calorie intake wasn't really sustaining me, so I ate half of my daughter's meal too. She didn't mind, she's a vegetarian and doesn't do calories. It was OK for a chain pub, (if that isn't a contradiction in terms) two meals for £8.99. I go for the fish, with tiny amount of chips and peas and two pints of watered down Carlsberg. All right, I take it back, not OK.

Eve, who is pretty observant for a typical teenager, whose head is constantly buried in an electronic device seventeen hours a day, sees a couple walking past the window.

Happy with pint in hand

'Did you see them Dad?'

'Who?' I say, wiping the remains of the fifth sachet of tartar sauce from my mouth, still desperate to ram as many calories into my bloodstream as possible.

'What's his name from the telly?'

'Usain Bolt?'

'No, you know.'

'Alan Partridge?'

'Dad mun!'

'OK, sorry... Peter Griffin? Neil Armstrong? Ghandi?'

'No!!! The police drama, in Welsh, you moron,' she screams.

I knew she meant *Hinterland* but I didn't see anyone.

'I'm sure it was them,' she insists.

'Which ones?'

'I don't know their names do I?'

'OK, do you mean DCI Mathias and Detective Sergeant Siân Owens?' I helpfully offer.

'Is that the blonde one Robbie was on about?' says Sue.

'Yeh them. They were walking hand in hand.'

'No, I'm sure it wasn't them,' I snigger knowingly.

Sunset, Pier

'Fancy some Rachel's Organic Yogurt for afters?' I ask.

'Get off your phone will you!'

'Did you know they are the largest employer in town?'

'No,' says Sue, 'But one thing I do know is that the mayor of Aberystwyth, who played Judith in *Life of Brian*, invited Michael Palin and Terry Jones to come watch the film in town.'

'Did they?'

'Yeh, I think so, Google didn't really say, lol.'

We go for a walk around town and watch the waves for a bit. It's a beautiful night. Then we pop into Tesco for a £3 Meal Deal, my breakie tomorrow.

We part company, I go to my hovel to whisper sweet nothings to my awesome Dawes bike that I never once doubted, while Sue and Eve retire to their four star, boutique Seaview Apartment (Ar Lan Y Mor), £55 a twin.

In my room the crap radiator has stopped working which means my wet clothes, that I'd been trying to dry, will be going back on wet in the morning. I think about leaving the window open to air the coat and get rid of some of the sweaty smell but think again. The seagulls are pretty hard around here (and noisy).

I'm in bed by 10:30pm, I manage some sleep (about half an hour) but then I suddenly do an *Aled* (after a 100 mile *Carten* a few years back) and jump out of bed in one leap, screaming like a baby due to severe cramp in my hamstring and calf. I stretch for twenty minutes then eat a Mars bar, hoping the sugar will help. I'm hopping around the room for about an hour before it eventually subsides and I can risk sleep.

Why am I doing this I ask myself again?

Cycling Stats

Start: 6:30am
Distance: 70.09 miles
Total Distance: 239.55 miles
Average Speed: 10.63mph
Fastest Speed: 30.90mph
Cycling Time: 6 hrs 35 mins
Finish: 5:30pm
Calories: 4730
Ascent: 5554 ft
Descent: 5534 ft
Beers: 2

Route

Hill Profile

 Day 6

Aberystwyth to Barmouth
Wednesday 3rd August 2016

iPhone alarm: Catch the Wind - Donovan

I wake at 6:30am with a bad stomach. Probably the unhealthy concoction of sugar-rich food and lager or maybe the effects of a smelly, mangy cell of a 'B' (no breakie) I find myself in?

I listen to Donovan for a bit while I check I don't still have cramp in my leg. It seems OK so I get up and check my panniers as per the daily, pre-ride ritual.

After yesterday's rain and wind I check the pretty useless BBC Weather app to see what I might have in store for me. I say useless because in Wales the weather is notoriously difficult to predict, especially with all the valleys and microclimates we have. Sometimes though I do wish the forecasters would look out the window in their office so they could see what they are saying is a load of crap!

Anyway, the outlook is good. Mostly cloudy, sunny intervals, a mixed bag really. Then I cast my eyes down to the black circles with pointy arrows at the bottom of the display. And the numbers are going up.

'Oh dear, wind. I bloody hate wind when I'm on a bike!' I say to no one in particular.

'Bloody Donovan. I picked that track because of yesterday, it wasn't an invitation for an encore you hippy!'

I visit Sue and Eve (at their exclusive pad) and we have a breakfast party of tea, stale cheese and ham roll, yogurt and orange juice. I save my Tesco delights for later.

My right knee is really sore, like someone is sticking a knife in it. I've had ligament trouble in that knee for a while but thought the exercise might help. I'm also really tired this morning.

I eventually set off, cruising through some side streets before hitting the A487. Soon my lungs are burning as I pedal up the big hill out of town. I pause for a moment to laugh at the National Library of Wales where more books are pulped than in a chapter of *Fahrenheit 451*. A friend who worked there told me they carry them out the back door and fill skips up just as quickly as they cart them in the front door. That's Literature Wales for you – a laughing stock!

I push on and get hassled by the busy traffic as I crawl slowly to the top of the hill. I'm knackered and sweaty by the time I pull over for a breather and let the impatient bastards pass.

Tip for the Top: Avoid Aberystwyth rush hour!

I get to thinking while I'm puffing and panting and stuffing an energy bar into my mouth at the same time. I've actually thought about this a lot since starting the trip. Why are people in such a rush to get to a job that they probably hate? Especially if it means driving so fast and recklessly that they almost kill the poor cyclist that is minding his own business just plodding slowly along, in no particular rush to get anywhere fast.

The good news about getting to the top of a hill of course is that sooner or later you're rewarded with a big downhill (unless you have crappy wheels on an old Dawes bike just outside Amroth).

I jump back on as the wind picks up. I drop down a few cogs and up the gears. Oh dear, this is a very fast downhill, quite dangerous in this wind as well. I wobble and weave a bit as a few idiots overtake me (even though I'm doing over 30mph) and their slipstream causes me to shake but I keep pedalling and enjoy the views over the common.

Windy Borth

I see a sign for Borth and think, oh my friend Helen lives there, I'll take a detour, maybe get a cup of tea. Then I remember I don't have her number.

I think about visiting the zoo, to see the lions, then stop for a look at the sea. My *Dawkins* that wind is strong! No way is that just 20mph as the forecast said. This is 35-40mph at least already! I move off and then realise as I'm hurtling down the main street that I'm not actually pedalling anymore, even though I'm picking up speed.

It's a strange little place, Borth. There's a very long beach with an ancient submerged forest visible at low tide where stumps of oak, pine, birch, willow and hazel have been preserved by the peat over 3,500 years ago.

I carry on, almost to the end of the headland, before turning inland (with the wind) and then back, side-on to the gale as I follow signs for Machynlleth. I pull off the road at the Dyfi Furnace, an old wood-burning structure that dates from 1755. The furnace was used to smelt iron ore, and the huge waterwheel would have powered a huge pair of bellows that supplied air during the process.

Dyfi Furnace

I stop for a photo and unwrap my chicken salad sandwich. It's only a moment before I'm once again pondering the lives of drivers as they speed past this rusty, old relic from a bygone age, on their way to work, to meet a lover, to church, Morrisons, or a car crash as I sip my orange Lucozade in the drizzle that wasn't forecasted. Then I start humming *Traffic* by The Stereophonics to myself.

There is also a pretty waterfall just upstream of the building, where the River Einion flows. I cycle to the RSPB nature reserve at Ynys-hir and then stop for a breather at the Osprey Centre. I thought I'd just finish my grub before I try to get some miles done when it starts to rain a little heavier. I shelter under a tree. Then it really starts to empty down so I move under some bigger trees, then it rains so hard I'm singing Bob Dylan to myself again! I find a wall and hug that. Bloody BBC! I shelter for twenty minutes and then when the rain finally eases off I push on to Machynlleth.

I look across the estuary of the River Dyfi at the Snowdonia National Park in the distance. Established in 1951, it covers 827 square miles, with Y Wyddfa, (1085m) the highest peak in England and Wales. In the southern part of the park is Cadair Idris (893m) and Aran Fawddwy (905m) plus some other monsters, or should that be Marilyns?

Southern Snowdonia

Anyway, the really important thing is I'm going around the coast (or most of it) so I'm not cycling over these bloody big mountains! I've walked over many of them over the years and that was tough enough so I reckon it's only fair I visit the seaside on this tour. Phew, sound convincing eh?

I cycle on for a few more miles and just as I get to town it starts to rain again. I hide under the clock tower and a nice, elderly lady asks where I'm going.

'Hello, well, I'm hoping to make Barmouth today,' I reply, as much in hope as anything.

'Did you get caught in the rain?' she asks, not the slightest bit fazed by my proposed distance.

'No, I missed it, thankfully.'

Machynlleth Clock Tower

'So are you doing this ride for anything?'

'Yeh, I'm cycling around Wales for charity,' I reply, undoing my waterproof to show off my homemade 'Wales Trails' t-shirt.

'Oh that's a good cause, I'll sponsor you,' she says as she wonders off to a local shop to get change of a twenty pound note.

'My husband was a paratrooper and he suffered with this in later life,' she continued.

Ah, I realise how meagre my mileage must have sounded now.

The lovely Mrs Jane Wykes gives me £5, wishes me well and goes on her way.

I'm thinking of spending a little time in the town that is famous for the nearby Bron-Yr-Aur cottage. The place where Jimmy Page and Robert Plant wrote the album Led Zeppelin III in 1970 but I'm aware of the winds reaching hurricane speeds if I'm not careful and the terrifying prospect of riding into them, back down the coast.

In addition to this, Machynlleth, a 5,000 year old, copper mining, Bronze Age town, has another special role in Welsh history because of its connection with Owain Glyndŵr, Prince of Wales, who rebelled against the English. He was crowned Prince of Wales in 1404 near the Parliament House, which is one of three medieval houses in town, in the presence of leaders from Scotland, France and Spain.

On 16 September 1400, Glyndŵr instigated the Welsh Revolt against the rule of Henry IV of England. The uprising was very successful and the Welsh rapidly gained control of large areas of the country, but it suffered from an inability to defend fortresses and coastlines due to lack of resources. Poor old Owain was driven from his last strongholds in 1409, but he avoided capture despite huge rewards offered. He was never betrayed to the English and no one really knows what happened to him but his death is recorded as 1415. Since then his name has achieved mythical status and he is regarded as a hero in Wales who will return to liberate his people when needed. I guess nobody thought to tell him about Thatcher or Cameron?

I pedalled on, following the route signs west, cycling into a headwind now. A good downhill sees me on a busy road near Pennal. I take a detour off the main road and end up in some hills above the road doing a pretty pointless circle or so it seemed at the time. I was tired, cycling into the wind, still annoyed at cars who seemed to think it was OK to speed past a bike at fifty or sixty miles an hour with a couple of feet to spare. I was frustrated at being forced to add miles just to avoid drivers who hadn't read their highway code when, as is often the case, something amazing happened.

Hurtling downhill on a quiet, country lane I spooked two goldfinches. They flew right in front of me and my spirits lifted immediately. But, even better was to come. As well as the adults there were two youngsters that followed. They were obviously smaller and struggled to keep up with their parents (or the older birds) pace and as I was *flying* at over 20mph myself I found them literally inches from my face! A truly remarkable view – eat your heart out Natural History Unit, Bristol, I was in my own episode of Supersense!

I soon re-join the main artery west and am back in the land of HGVs and English tourists who slow down for sheep on the opposite side of the road but speed up when they see a Dawes bike! It's then I notice a black Kia with Scooby Doo stickers as it passes me by. I stop for a quick chat to Sue and Eve who are off to Barmouth to look for a campsite for the three of us.

Stormy seas, Aberdyfi

I meet up with the family at Aberdyfi (or Aberdovey as the English say) and have a quiet half hour rest from the

wind. I manage to consume a sandwich, chicken tikka sausage roll thing from the Spar and a nice half of lager at the Britannia Inn. I even take my jacket off and think about going 'top-off' as the sun comes out and the breeze drops for a bit.

Aberdyfi is a lovely seaside town but like so many places in Wales, especially on the coast, an influx of foreigners has pushed up property prices and changed the demographic of the area. Now, only 38% of the town class themselves as Welsh!

The town is famously linked to the 'Welsh Atlantis' legend Cantre'r Gwaelod and the bells of St Peter's church often play 'The Bells of Aberdovey'. There are also other bell-related projects in town that connect to the story.

Suitably refreshed I get back on my bike and hope the girls find a nice comfy place to sleep tonight in Barmouth. My hopes are not high when I consider how many English tourists I see and hear wandering around the area though.

Magic Lantern Cinema, Tywyn

I cycle partly with the wind, partly against it as I head towards Tywyn. I make good progress by twisting my body and 'tacking' into and out of the wind like a latter day Henry Morgan.

I look at my Google Maps app on my iPhone and a random page out of an old Aldi's Road Atlas that I tore out for just such an occasion and see what looks like an exciting route over the mountain towards Barmouth.

I decide to take it but after a few big hills I begin to have doubts. The wind is picking up again and I'm struggling to make progress up a deserted country lane. I stop to ask a farmer, who's cutting his hedge, if there is a good road further on up but he only speaks Welsh. He calls his son, who I quickly spell out my journey to. I also try to impress upon him the fact that I'm also Welsh, albeit shy of God's language in this lifetime. The last thing I'd want is a helpful local to think I'm a foreigner and direct me over the precipice into a forgotten prehistoric world and the fiery volcano below.

Stunning scenery

The farmer's son convinces me it's not such a good idea to continue on up, especially with the high winds and also points out that the tracks are now harder to distinguish since the contractors have put in new roads to build wind turbines on the mountain. I know what he means having got lost above Hirwaun, heading for Neath, a year back with Derek on our mountain bikes. I heed local knowledge and whizz back down the hill to the main road. I know how remote and wild the terrain around Cadair Idris is so decide I don't really want to take my trusty Dawes anywhere near that today.

I cycle on but stop frequently to take several photos, such is the beauty of the countryside. The scenery along this section of Welsh coastline is rugged and spectacular. I pause again to breathe in the air, admire the dry stone wall building and can't help notice the white horses out to sea. The wind is picking up again and the waves with it. I decide it best to pedal on up the coast as best I can and hope the gale doesn't change direction, as it's more or less with me at the moment.

Near Llangelynin

I'm following the A493 main road, which is very pleasant, and fairly car free. Down below is the picturesque railway, the Cambrian Coast Line, which runs from Aberystwyth to Pwllheli right up the west coast of Wales. I feel totally alone now, at peace with the natural world. Just the low rumble of the wind off the sea, the clickety-clack of the odd train that passes beneath me and the reassuring sound of my spinning wheels. It's a good time and I'm happy. Just the sort of complacent *happy* that can be quickly spoilt by a sudden puncture or the tell-tale noise of a spoke pinging. I pray to the god of cyclists that my new hybrid machine will keep me safe and deliver me from the evil of a rusty nail or a sharp piece of glass.

I continue up the coast for a while then slowly head east and inland towards the village of Llwyngwril. Now in my experience, whenever you're travelling around any country, occasionally you happen upon something remarkable.

Maybe you arrive in Malaga and it's their annual fireworks display, maybe you book a backpackers next door to where Osama bin Laden blows up an embassy in Dar es Salaam, maybe you miss the riots in Jakarta because you're so drunk in a Michael Jackson lookalike, karaoke bar that you miss your taxi home? Maybe you decide to get off the train at a small village in Portugal and discover it's hosting the biggest festa of the year, the president is in town and the secret service start eyeing you up in your hippy clothes and hefty camera bag?

Getting to know the locals

The expression being in the right place at the right time springs to mind, or sometimes the wrong place... Like the time me and Sue were at a temple in Luxor, Egypt, a few weeks before Al Qaeda butchered a load of tourists there. We decided there were too many bad vibes and so left and went back to our camels.

Well, this was one of those rare moments. Here I was cycling around my own country for charity and I just happen to stop for a drink of water. I might have cycled through and missed it but Buddha was thirsty. The village is eerily quiet. Deserted. Well, almost... Then my sixth sense kicks in, something weird is happening here.

Some creative sparks had decided to yarn bomb the place! All over the streets of this small coastal village in Gwynedd were woolly things. The Llwyngwril Yarn Bombers had created the most amazing street art by knitting around trees, park benches and lampposts.

I stopped to chat to some locals but unfortunately I was held back slightly by the language barrier again. I made a note to add 'learn yarn' to my things to do before I die list.

Swap Shop my Dawes?

The project was launched to raise money for the local community centre - Y Ganolfan Llwyngwril. There is also a knitted trail around Llwyngwril that tells the story of Gwril the Giant along the way.

Of course, this being Wales, the knitters have been battling against the weather since they started. Wool, wind and rain don't mix and the exhibits can become a little

95

soggy. But when the sun comes out again the townsfolk spring back to life.

In a way I'm glad I arrive half way through my safari because if I'd have stumbled upon this knitted bike on Newgale beach I would have done a crafty Noel Edmunds and been on my way, leaving the old Discovery behind and tied to a lamp post.

Is it me or are the Welsh just mental?

Barmouth Railway Viaduct

Back on the Dawes I almost freewheel, such is the strength of the wind blowing me along the coast, and make good time to Arthog. I then realise I've missed the railway line crossing so double back. It's actually quite difficult to find and not signposted at all. I just used guesswork and then asked a local family on their bikes that looked like two miles was as much as they'd manage in a day. I guessed they'd come from Barmouth and so I headed down a small lane until I picked up a trail sign again.

I start to cross the Barmouth Bridge but it's so windy that the sand from the estuary is blown into my eyes blinding me. The wind must be nearly 45-50mph now and cycling is hard so I decide to push and take some photos instead.

The ever-changing patterns formed in the sand are wonderful to watch and I waste a few minutes leaning over the side of the bridge. The shortcut this bridge across the River Mawddach affords is very welcome though, especially after more than fifty miles of hard but enjoyable riding.

The bridge first opened in 1867, although in 1980 woodworm threatened its safety. The bridge is a Grade II listed structure, and at 700m is one of the longest timber viaducts still in regular use in Britain.

Sand 'Etch A Sketch'

I cycled off the bridge, up a short but steep hill and then down the road into town. I dropped down to the harbour then did a lap of the sights before sending Sue a text to see where we'd be sleeping that night.

I was now sat outside the Tilman pub (which I assumed was named after the famous English mountaineer and sailor, Bill Tilman, who used to live in the town) with half a lager in my hand, pleased that once again the revamped bike had done me proud. I had just asked the not so friendly barmaid if they had any rooms in the pub but just got a scowl for my troubles. I poked my tongue out when she turned away to top up my drink.

Barmouth grew up around the shipbuilding industry, and more recently as a seaside resort for Brummies as it's one of the closest resorts to the landlocked West Midlands, with a high proportion of visitors coming from Wolverhampton, Birmingham, Dudley and other parts of the Black Country. William Wordsworth visited the town in the 19th Century and was well impressed but I doubt he'd like it much now. I get a reply from Sue.

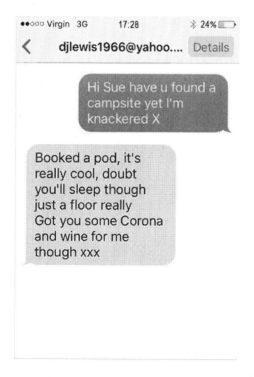

●●○○○ Virgin 3G   17:28   ✳ 24% ▭

<   djlewis1966@yahoo....   Details

Hi Sue have u found a campsite yet I'm knackered X

Booked a pod, it's really cool, doubt you'll sleep though just a floor really Got you some Corona and wine for me though xxx

Sue and Eve pick me up in the jeep and we drive about two or three miles out of town. It's a campsite but there are also 'pods', which are basically a really cool-looking shed with a door. Anyway, it was the last room at the inn, anywhere, such was the demand for accommodation on a windy Wednesday in north west Wales so Sue and Eve snapped it up. Not sure it was worth the £55 a night for basically a hard wooden floor but beggars can't be choosers.

Yes, it's trendy but we still have to pull out all the camping kit from the car to spread over the floor in order to make a bed of sorts to kip on.

'How much? For a shed!'

I shower, unpack, repack (usual ritual) and mentally prepare for a tough day tomorrow. I decide not to look at the weather app on the iPhone because it's bound to be positive, which will then be wrong and hence I'll get annoyed at the BBC again. In fact, maybe I've found the answer. Just avoid having anything to do with the BBC from now on. Just watch the music documentaries on BBC Four, the rugby coverage of the Six Nations, a bit of nature, spot of history, great science... OK, forget I said it. I'll just stop watching politics and the news.

We're not sure if there is a pub nearby for food so we drive back into town. Me and Eve visit a Co-op while Sue orders a Chinese takeaway. We visit a local pub for a pint of lager while we're waiting. It's OK, if a bit rough and unfriendly. We then pick up the rice, noodles, more noodles, chips, vegetable curry, more noodles and wonder why we didn't order meat or why I like noodles so much?

Back at the pod we devour the lot and wash it down with some Corona lager and wine. I'm knackered, so quickly fall asleep while Eve watches TV until the early hours now that she's on teenager time. I wake up in the early hours, can't get back to sleep because the hard wooden floor is so uncomfortable, even with the camping mats and sleeping bags, and get up and pack my bike.

Cycling Stats

Start: 8:30am
Distance: 55.83 miles
Total Distance: 295.38 miles
Average Speed: 11.08mph
Fastest Speed: 33.32mph
Cycling Time: 5 hrs 02 mins
Finish: 6:00pm
Calories: 3596
Ascent: 3399 ft
Descent: 3264 ft
Beers: 2
Wine: 1

Route

Hill Profile

 Day 7

Barmouth to Caernarfon
Thursday 4th August 2016

iPhone alarm: Wild is the Wind – David Bowie

Cows

Slept a few hours but the last few nights I've been waking in agony with a pain in my lower back and a stabbing pain in my groin. I assume it's just the long hours on a saddle, hard floors or maybe a recurrence of a varicocele I had when I was younger. A varicocele is an abnormal enlargement of the pampiniform venous plexus in the scrotum. In other words, a dodgy blood vessel in the bollock. I need to get it looked at when I return as if it's on the right side in someone over forty (I've got both sides and I'm fifty) it may be renal cancer. On that happy note I decide to do what most men do, not think about it and carry on, although I think I will need to get checked out when I get back.

I'm up by 6:00am to stretch and the pains soon go. We have a chocolate pastry thing, a strawberry yogurt and some orange juice for breakie.

I double-check my panniers and say goodbye to the ladies before shouting above the roar of the wind.

'Please don't book a bloody wooden shed again!'

I'm on the road again and soon pass a field full of llamas. Next is a field full of pretty cows. I stop for a photo and think that maybe this is nature's way of telling me to be a vegetarian again.

Awesome beach

I push on to Harlech where 51% of the people still speak Welsh despite Edward I's attempt to crush the Celts. The town is famous for Harlech Castle, which was built between 1282-89 as part of his 'Ring of Iron', before being captured by Owain Glyndŵr in 1404. It then became Glyndŵr's headquarters for the remainder of his uprising until English forces recaptured it in 1409.

During the 15th Century Wars of the Roses, the Lancastrians held Harlech for seven years, before Yorkist troops forced its surrender in 1468, a siege memorialised in the song Men of Harlech. What they would have thought about seeing llamas in fields though I don't know.

103

During the English Civil War in 1642, the castle was held by forces loyal to Charles I, until 1647 when it became the last fortification to surrender to Cromwell's Roundheads.

I stop for a quick recce of the castle, it's shut, as I'm a bit early. I take a photo in the horrible grey morning and pedal on.

Harlech Castle

The weather is not good. It's cold and damp. The wind is deciding what to do today and it's still quite dark. Ah well, it is August – the height of summer in Wales I think to myself for the seventh day on the trip to date. I was hoping to take my waterproof jacket off today but so far it's stayed zipped up tight.

My back pain has eased but my knees are killing me again. I don't like to give in so early in the day but there is nothing for it, I resort to drugs, a bit like Lance Armstrong but on a much smaller and more manageable scale.

I take two purple pills and wash them down with some of Aldi's finest Lucozade substitute. I take a photo because I quite like the colour of the tablets against the background of my black cycling mitt and figure if I cycle off the edge of a cliff in the next twenty minutes then if someone looks at my camera's images they'll know why.

I pedal on and soon the effects of the isobutylphenylpropanoic acid start to kick in. I pass a school or something (it's all a bit of a blur to be honest) and I see an orange and yellow dragon. I know this is Wales and that dragons are everywhere but in the middle of town on a damp Thursday? And it's massive as they say in Pontypridd!

Purple Pills

The oldest recorded use of the dragon to symbolise Wales is in the Historia Brittonum, written around AD 829. The book talks about the settlement of Britain by Trojan expatriates and states that Britain took its name after Brutus, a Turk. This work was also used by Geoffrey of Monmouth who gave us a lot of the King Arthur and Merlin stuff.

Personally I think this modern British history is irrelevant as we know modern humans have inhabited Wales for at least 29,000 years. Hunter-gatherers also came here from Central Europe, after the last ice age over 10,000 years ago, and have been here ever since.

When the climate changed and sea levels rose Wales and Ireland became separated by the Irish Sea. The historian John Davies reckoned that the story of Cantre'r

Gwaelod's drowning might be linked to distant folk memories of this time.

Anyway, the fact is I took some pills and saw a dragon in the street, which freaked me out. And it wasn't knitted either.

These days of course the red dragon is seen as symbolising all things Welsh. So why was this one orange?

I think I saw this?

Still under the influence of the mysterious purple pills I cycled on, up and around the various branches of the Afon Dwyryd until I eventually happen upon a weird, *Lord of the Rings* type kingdom a mile or two off the road, overlooking the sea.

I stop to admire the castle then whizz downhill, only braking for the speed bumps, before I arrive at the entrance of the Mediterranean-style complex of Portmeirion. I exchange a few pleasantries with David the gatekeeper (not Zuul the Gatekeeper of Gozer by the way) who very kindly allows me in to the grounds to take photographs.

This amazing place was designed by Sir Clough Williams-Ellis, who constructed the village between 1925 and 1975. He incorporated fragments of demolished buildings and included works by many other architects.

Magic colours

Portmeirion is now owned by a charitable trust, has a hotel, together with shops, a cafe, tearoom, and restaurant. It's a top tourist attraction in north Wales and a ticket to visit costs about £11. Unless you're pals with David the gatekeeper like me of course.

The village of Portmeirion has, over the years, inspired many an artist and played host to a number of famous people. Noël Coward wrote Blithe Spirit here and architect Frank Lloyd Wright visited in 1956. Gregory Peck, Ingrid Bergman and Paul McCartney have also popped by.

As you can imagine many TV programmes and films have been shot here because it's just so wacky. Dr Who, Citizen Smith and a Siouxsie and the Banshees video to name but a few.

Of course, the most well known association with Portmeirion is Patrick McGoohan's cult-TV series The Prisoner. Between 1966-67 intelligence agent 'Number 6' was locked up and interrogated here. Fans have flocked here ever since, including Stephen Fry, Hugh Laurie, Jools Holland, Iron Maiden and XTC.

There is also a Prisoner-themed souvenir shop in what was McGoohan's home. Many of the locations used in the series are virtually unchanged after more than forty years.

A prisoner in a cycling helmet

I would have liked to stay longer (and no doubt next time I visit I'll bring my proper camera) but there was lots more to see and do in north Wales so I had to jump back in the time machine and press the button.

Me and Sue came here over twenty years ago, in the rain. I don't remember much of that visit, I probably had toothache or something, but this time I'm surrounded by strange kaleidoscope colours and there's magic in the air. I will have to ask Sue what she packed in my medicine kit. I thought purple was Ibuprofen? Whatever they were my knees are still sore.

I cycle on, alongside the sea, the railway and soon I'm in Porthmadog. I watch the steam trains come and go for a bit, it starts raining and I shelter near the tourist information centre. Then I hear the familiar sound of the sexy Shirley Manson, when she was with Angelfish, singing

You Can Love Her from the most amazing album ever! It's my mobile ringtone.

Impressive gardens

'Hi Sue, where are you?' I ask.

'Hello? I'm after a website for my window cleaning business.'

'Sorry Sue, what did you say? The steam train's whistle was blowing.'

'I don't want a huge site, just a web presence really, hello?'

'Oh dear, sorry, Dave Lewis, Web Design Wales here, I thought you were my missus, sorry mate.'

'That's OK, so how much then?'

'I'm actually cycling around Wales now...'

The conversation is a bit surreal but eventually we have a chat about me designing a website when I get back down south.

Porthmadog is another interesting town though. The town grew as a port exporting slate to England and around the world. Nowadays it relies mainly on tourism. It's easy to get to Snowdonia and it has the cool railway.

There are some very special individuals to come from this part of the world, especially from the nearby villages of Morfa Bychan and Tremadog.

One of the UK's greatest heroes was born at Tremadog in 1888, although his father was Irish and his mother Scottish. Thomas Edward Lawrence, better known as Lawrence of Arabia, became a legend throughout the world, after his incredible role in the Arab Revolt of 1916 and for his vivid writings about his experiences.

Looking stormy

Morfa Bychan on the other hand was the home of David Owen, an 18th Century blind harpist. He died at the age of twenty-nine in 1741 and tradition has it that as he lay on his death bed he called for his harp and composed the beautiful air *Dafydd y Garreg Wen*.

Also from the village is Caspa, the nine-year-old llama. He recently set a Guinness World Record by jumping almost four feet over a hurdle.

In Porthmadog I rendezvous with Sue and Eve for the last time though. We meet up near the train station.

The Ffestiniog railway is roughly thirteen miles long and runs from the harbour at Porthmadog to the slate mining town of Blaenau Ffestiniog, travelling through superb forests and imposing mountain scenery. It is the oldest surviving railway company in the world, although not the oldest railway.

This is where I say goodbye to my support team. Something other expeditions (I'm thinking Ewan and Charley) would never travel without, wimps.

Must say though it was great having Sue and Eve, and the car for a few days, especially when the old bike broke and I needed to get a lift to Cardigan to have it re-built.

Ffestiniog Railway Company

I stock up on isotonic drinks and ask Sue where my little plastic container of oil is?

'Oil?'

'Yes, oil,' I reply.

'Was it in a small, black, dog poop bag?'

'Yeh, that's the one, where is it?'

'Oh, I didn't know what it was so I left it in the house in St Dogmaels.'

'Guess my chain can survive without oil for another week then.'

What did I say about a support crew?

It's a quick goodbye (I hate long goodbyes) and off I cycle down the high street. No matter I think to myself, my buttie Mark will be here any minute. He promised to bring his son Dan, Finn the boxer dog and Robbie our mate up

111

north to meet me for a few beers. He'll probably have bike oil with him anyway.

Mark wants to tour the castles of this rugged part of Wales and our mate Robbie was going to put his bike on the car to cycle with me for a couple of days. I can't wait, cycling alone is good, it gives you time to think, to chill out, clear the mind, especially after a couple of purple pills, but it's also great to have company when doing a trip like this. Good to share the road with kindred spirits, like Warren and Yago, although those days seem like a lifetime ago now.

I pedal on to Criccieth Castle, a native Welsh castle situated on the headland of a rocky peninsula overlooking Tremadog Bay. A great spot for a castle I must say. It was built by Llywelyn the Great but was heavily modified by, yep, you've guessed it, the English forces of Edward I in the late 13th Century. What is it with that bloke and castles? He'd have therapy today.

Approaching Criccieth

In 1404 the castle was re-captured by Owain Glyndŵr and the walls still bear scorch marks from the battle. Criccieth was also used by the famous artist and snuff-sniffer, J. M. W. Turner, as one of the locations for his famous series of paintings depicting shipwrecked sailors.

112

I pause for a photo. Then I finish a half eaten energy bar and have a tricky decision to make. I was planning to cycle down to Pwllheli on the Llŷn peninsula. Historically, the peninsula is important as a pilgrimage route to Bardsey Island, and its relative isolation has helped to conserve the Welsh language and culture.

This remoteness has also been the area's downfall as foreigners have since moved in. Holiday homes remain a bone of contention among locals, many of who can't afford to buy a house anymore. It was for this reason that during the 1970s (up to the 1990s), a group known as Meibion Glyndŵr started burning down holiday homes, many of them on Llŷn.

If I'd had more time I would have cycled to the end of the peninsula and this area of outstanding natural beauty but a headwind, a long day on Ynys Môn tomorrow, the tempting prospect of a good trail (Route 8) and a hot bath in Caernarfon persuaded me to cut across country instead.

Rugged landscape

I leave Criccieth and pause halfway up a big hill out of town as my chain slips off. I fix it quickly but sit down on the pavement to eat my sandwiches. After the hill I'm soon enjoying nice rolling roads until I reach the busy A487. I only stay on this road for a couple of miles before turning off onto Route 8 (Lôn Eifion) for a fantastic trail most of the way to Caernarfon.

The mist comes down not long after heading cross-country but at least the rain holds off. I'm once again enjoying a remote and peaceful landscape. I'm sweating like a pig and still stuffing calories in like there's no tomorrow though.

I'm not far from Caernarfon now and quite excited about seeing the *Ponty* gang. I text Mark to find out where he is. He rings me back.

'You'll never believe this...'

'Go on,' I reply.

'Well, I was going to get money out of the cashpoint machine for the trip when smoke started coming out of the wall and it ate my bank card! There was a major problem with the bank. It took my card. Honest. It did. You won't believe this but it swallowed my card. I was just going to get money. And I've had a bit of hassle as well...'

'Women trouble?'

'Aye, don't ask, and Robbie's bike is knackered, and guess who's not talking to me (again) and I don't know if Finn would be allowed in the castles and my cashpoint card got swallowed up and...' (repeat three times)

'So are you coming?'

'Well I was going to but I've got no cash now, the machine took my card and the bank said it'll take three days to get a new one and...'

'So you're not coming?'

'Well I would have but the bank...'

'What about Robbie?'

'Well I was going to give him a lift, he's skint, and we can't afford it, and my Facebook account got hacked (again), and my bike is crap anyway and Finn is starving, I have to buy him food and I haven't got a bank card...'

'So, are you coming or not?'

'I'll try to come tomorrow but...'

I guess I'm seeing north Wales alone then. Ah well, I guessed as much anyway.

I make it to town, still pretty much on cycle trails, do a lap of the castle, take a few photos, impressed by the sheer size and forbidding presence of the building. There are Welsh flags everywhere and I feel very patriotic. Foreign tourists, from all over Europe are everywhere and I'm thinking this must be good for the local economy. Then I stop for a second outside The Anglesey Arms pub, down by the sea. I was going to sit in the sun and have a pint but then I hear this Irish folk singer droning on about the mountains of bloody Mourne or some shit. Bloody hell, this is Wales, we have Snowdonia here, we're not interested in the bleedin' view from the Skerries are we? Who hired this guy? I mean, think about it. Do you go to Ireland and hear Welsh male voice choirs on every street corner? Do you listen to Catatonia cover bands in the bars? I skip the pint and hope it dents their profits so much they go bust!

Caernarfon Castle

Suitably fed up I cycle across the bridge and look across the sea to Ynys Môn. I wonder what tomorrow will bring as I'm about half way around Wales now.

Caernarfon has been inhabited since prehistoric times and Celtic tribes were still living here when the Romans came and built a fort in AD 80. In the 11th Century William the Conqueror tried to conquer the Welsh but failed. It wasn't until Llywelyn ap Gruffudd refused to lick Edward I's boots that the trouble really started. After finally conquering the Welsh, in May 1283, the construction of the castle was started a month later.

The castles of Caernarfon, Conwy and Harlech were the most impressive of their time in Wales, and their construction, along with a number of other castles in the country, helped establish English rule.

An interesting fact surrounding the building of the castle was the discovery of the body of Roman emperor Magnus Maximus at Caernarfon, which Edward I ordered to be buried in a local church. I bet he did a lot of ordering. He seems the type doesn't he?

Town centre

I find my digs for the night, the fantastic Totters Hostel, just down a side street from the castle. I was greeted by a lovely Dutch lady who shows me around. I get a bed in a four-bed dorm, although I only end up sharing the room with a young Italian lad. I go through the ritual of pannier organisation, I charge my electronic equipment, my iPhone, my camera battery and my Garmin bike computer. Then I stand in the shower for ages and realise it's one of my earliest finishes yet, about 4:00pm. Maybe I should have gone to Pwllheli after all?

I have a long day ahead next so I get my head down for a quick kip before going for a stroll around town. I debate what tea should be for a few minutes before finally settling on the carbohydrate and fat-packed snack of chips, curry and mince beef pie washed down with a pint of lager and topped off with a Wispa chocolate bar.

The town is remarkably quiet now, all the tourists have disappeared and I chat to some locals for a bit who tell me there is nothing here, no work, nothing.

'You've got the castle though,' I try to cheer them up.

'Yeh, but you can only look at it so many times.'

'Fair point, I know what you mean, I have the Old Bridge and *the red thing*, hwyl fawr.'

One thing the town does have is the largest percentage of Welsh language speakers anywhere in Wales though, so that's good. The castle and town walls are a World Heritage Site too. I compare this to my hometown of Pontypridd. We have a bridge, a park, 'The Wonky' and a good rugby team.

I rang Sue and explained that Mark and Robbie probably wouldn't make it now and that I would be on my own for the rest of the journey. She told me they'd just got back home and she'd discovered that her bank account had been hacked and almost a thousand pounds had been spent on goods and flights. I said it would be all right and the bank would surely reimburse her, especially as the purchases weren't even in Wales. Worse news was that Charlie the gerbil was ill. Eve was upset as she'd only just lost Keith a few months before.

I sit in the TV lounge of the hostel and surf the net on my phone for a bit. I discover that Edward II (the gay one) was born at Caernarfon Castle in 1284 and created Prince of Wales in 1301. His nasty dad said that he should control all of Wales and its incomes. Since then the eldest son of the English monarch has traditionally held this title. I think that's Prince Charles now? Don't really go in for this royalty stuff much, although how they got where they are is quite interesting. Mostly through violence, oppression, greed and war I guess.

The castle building of Edward I was pretty OCD though. He built the castles, his 'Ring of Iron' as it was called, in order to defeat the Welsh princes between 1276 and 1295. Some of the most famous, and well preserved are Beaumaris, Caernarfon, Conwy, Denbigh, Flint, Harlech and Rhuddlan. His building programme would have cost about £30 million in todays money so a mere bagatelle really. Just goes to show how cheap slave labour was then. The Millennium Stadium cost £121 million in comparison.

Sue texts to say she's found me a guest house in Bangor for £30 a night, I ring the owner to confirm, watch some TV, swear at the news and the usual biased coverage then phone Mam for a chat before I retire early to bed at 10:30pm.

Cycling Stats

Start: 6:30am
Distance: 42.04 miles
Total Distance: 337.42 miles
Average Speed: 10.12mph
Fastest Speed: 27.05mph
Cycling Time: 4 hrs 09 mins
Finish: 4:00pm
Calories: 2576
Ascent: 2611 ft
Descent: 2671 ft
Beers: 1

Route

Hill profile

 # Day 8

Caernarfon to Bangor
Friday 5th August 2016

iPhone alarm: Everyday is a Winding Road – Sheryl Crow

Up by 5:00am, crept out of the dorm so as not to wake up the snoring Roman in the bed opposite. I go downstairs in the hostel and make tea, wholemeal toast and jam. I try to eat the world's biggest bowl of cornflakes for breakfast as well. I did the washing up, as is expected, then quietly tiptoed back upstairs to pack my bike for the day.

Got slightly lost trying to find the Route 8 signs and ended up doing a lap of the harbour before finding the trail out of town.

Peaceful and still

The Lôn Las Menai is only four miles long but is a great little trail. It's also part of the Lôn Las Cymru. The route I'll be taking today (Route 8), part of the National Cycle Network, running through the heart of the country from the capital city, Cardiff, in the south, to Holyhead, my destination by dinnertime today, on the far west of Ynys Môn in the north. Although 250 miles long with some on-road sections much of the route follows old railway lines, such as Lôn Las Menai, Lôn Eifion, the Mawddach Trail and the Taff Trail. A road bike with racing tyres will struggle on the rougher surfaces but a hybrid should be fine. I hoped my customised model would continue to serve me well.

Ynys Môn so close!

As I cycle up the coast I'm struck by how peaceful the morning is, how the water is so still and Ynys Môn so close, just across the sea. You'd swear you could swim across in five minutes.

I pedal close to the main road and have to negotiate the traffic heading for the Britannia Bridge. This is a bit of a nightmare, especially around rush hour, but the trail takes me to the older bridge, which is so much nicer.

The Menai Suspension Bridge also carries road traffic between the island of Môn and the mainland of Wales. The bridge was designed by Thomas Telford, the Scottish engineer, nice guy and all-round genius, who completed the bridge in 1826.

I make a mental note of the pub just before the bridge for the return journey and take a few photos. I push the bike across on the right-hand side and look forward to a good day's cycling on a mostly flat island.

Menai Suspension Bridge

I pause half way across the bridge, I look at the light shining on the water, it's beautiful. I'm really happy and looking forward to the day.

Then Sue texts – Charlie Watts died, Eve's gerbil not the Stones drummer of course, Keith Richards went almost six months back. I'm nearly 100 feet above the Menai Straits, the views are stunning, heavenly you might even say. Then my daughter Eve rings to talk about death.

I'm suddenly thrown into despair. I was up, now I'm down. I can't help think it's so strange how life does this to you so often. I chat to Eve for a while then I have to be moving on.

I leave the bridge and I'm back on solid ground again. I'm on Ynys Môn at last. Fifty years old and it's taken me this long. I'm almost embarrassed. Then I remember that I have been here before but that was after our Irish ferry detoured there in storms after an old rugby trip. We drove across in the snow. I didn't see much that time.

View from a bridge

Ynys Môn (or Anglesey) is 276 square miles, the largest island of Wales, although it only has a population of 70,000 people.

Numerous megalithic monuments (giant stones) and menhirs (standing stones) are present on the island as well as twenty-eight cromlechs (stone circles) so there were humans here tens of thousands of years ago.

Historically, Ynys Môn has long been associated with druids. The Romans first invaded in AD 60 but it took until AD 78 before the island was completely occupied due to Boudica's revolt down south that distracted the pesky Italians.

Boudica was queen of the British Celtic Iceni tribe who led an uprising against the occupying forces of the Roman Empire. The story goes that when her husband, who was an ally of Rome, died, his will was ignored. Boudica was flogged, her daughters raped, and Roman financiers took over the kingdom.

This was a bit much for our heroine who apparently was very tall, with fierce eyes and a harsh voice. She had a great mass of the reddest hair that fell down to her hips. Her appearance was terrifying. I think I married one of her descendants.

Tranquil island

Anyway, she took her chance when the Roman Emperor was away trying to conquer Ynys Môn in AD 60. She led the Iceni (her own tribe), the Trinovantes (the most powerful Celtic tribe), and other Britons in revolution. They destroyed Colchester causing the Romans to abandon their quest in Ynys Môn and return to defend London.

Boudica led 100,000 mental Celtic warriors who burned and destroyed much of the Roman settlements of the south east, killing 80,000 before the Romans regrouped and finally defeated the Britons in the Midlands somewhere.

Emperor Nero was so worried by the Celts that he even considered withdrawing all Roman forces from Britain. Boudica then apparently poisoned herself rather than be captured.

So first the Romans came, then Irish pirates, then the Vikings, then Saxons, then Normans and finally 'Longshanks' of course. Nowadays it's property developers and second-home buyers from England who are swallowing up the old Welsh ways like the Chinese in Tibet, or Coca Cola in Cuba. United Nations anyone?

I cycled on. The plan was to follow Route 8 out to Holyhead, then Route 5 back so at least I saw more of the island than my mate Aled did when he sped across with Derek a few years back. All they saw were lanes.

I stop for a photo at the famous train station of: Llanfairpwllgwyngyllgogerychwyrndrobwllllantysiliogogogoch. Try saying that after a few real ales or some purple pills!

Railway building

The 6,000-year-old village of Llanfairpwllgwyngyll is also known as Llanfairpwll, Llanfair PG, Veganville, or Llanfair-pwllgwyngyll-gogery-chwyrn-drobwll-llan-tysilio-gog o-goch.

The long form of the name was invented by the Victorians for promotional purposes in the 1860s and is the longest place name in Europe and the second longest official one-word place name in the world. The longest goes to a small hill near Hawkes Bay in New Zealand: Taumatawhakatangi-hangakoauauotamatea-turipukakapiki maunga-horonukupokaiwhen-uakitanatahu, which Tennis star Martina Navratilova learned to say when she was ten years old.

In 2015, Channel 4 Welsh weatherman Liam Dutton pronounced the full name of the Welsh village during a live forecast. Within twenty-four hours of being uploaded to YouTube the video of the pronunciation had accumulated well over five million views.

Phonetic version too

I still can't say the long version of Llanfair PG, although my friend Neil Topping could say it when he was about ten years old too. Translated it means 'St Marys Church in the hollow of the white hazel near to the rapid whirlpool of Llantysilio of the red cave'. Personally I couldn't care less about being able to say it. I have enough trouble with much smaller words so don't want to drown people in phlegm just for a party trick.

The gift shop was shut which was a shame as I was dying to see the creative ways that they could incorporate a name that long onto a tea towel or a four inch beermat. Never mind, I cycle on and stop at a Co-op to get a meal deal.

After an hour or more of cycling I begin to realise what Aled said about lanes. Lanes, lanes and more lanes in fact! Still, it's mostly flat, the views across the sea are fantastic although it looks like it's raining on the mountains of Snowdonia.

Another hour (through lanes) and I'm beginning to relax a bit after the shock of learning about poor Charlie. I start to daydream again. Then I stop and take my iPhone out to write some notes (using the Notes app) and come over all poetic again.

House martins hawking
over Ynys Môn fields
Y Wyddfa grey across the water

Snowdonia from Ynys Môn

I pedal on, slowly clocking up the miles as I head to Holyhead. After a while I have to give in and admit that the island is not the most exciting of places. Still, it's very...

still. Peaceful, quiet. Why am I complaining? I like all these things.

Then suddenly without warning this all changes. I'm happily speeding down a rare hill when a big, fat bumblebee flies into my head. Not just my head mind you but my helmet. It gets stuck. I'm picking up speed, 20mph, 25mph, the bee is buzzing, it's going to sting me soon. Oh dear, what if I'm allergic to bee stings? What if I die of anaphylactic shock in a quiet lane? That's no way for an intrepid explorer like me to go out. A combine harvester, an avalanche, a grizzly bear, a pack of wild sheep painted pink yes, but not an insect!

I feel something sticking in my scalp, have I been stung already? I wait for the rapid onset of symptoms, the itchy rash, the throat and tongue swelling, shortness of breath (I had that anyway), the vomiting of half a meal deal, a poet's light-headedness and low blood pressure (no, definitely high at the moment).

I decide to use one hand to take the helmet off while one hand keeps firm hold of the unstable, pannier-clad bike as I hurtle down this country lane with rapidly approaching potholes and the distant sound of a tractor coming up the road.

I take it back. Ynys Môn is an exciting place.

I manage to unbuckle the helmet with my left hand. I take it off, shake it by my side and the bee escapes unhurt. Bang! Pothole. I nearly lose it as I wobble and quickly slap the helmet back on my head. Right, need to do up the strap now. I try for a few minutes, hand playing do up the strap like one of those annoying, fluffy monkey's hitting a drum.

I eventually stop as the road flattens out and I can safely apply the brakes.

'Bloody lanes!'

I push on further west and feel a bit like Willard as he's sucked up the river to Kurtz. I was on a mission now. Get to Holyhead at all costs. Take the photo and get back on the bike and retrace the route back to the bridge, cross to the safety of Bangor on a Friday night, get tea and medals, then sleep soundly knowing the journey is over half way through. OK, maybe a bit too dramatic for these peaceful country lanes but you get the picture.

I cross a few small bridges and take photos of the canals. It's still quite flat which is great for the knees. They're not as sore as they have been but my bum is pretty numb now instead. My neck and shoulders are fairly stiff too. Seized up pretty bad actually, but I carry on.

Eventually I reach what looks like an abandoned airfield (except it isn't). This is RAF Valley. I see signs saying that I'm entering MOD property and that I'll be shot or arrested if I trespass or take photos. I take some photos.

RAF Valley provides advanced pilot training using BAE Hawk T2 aircraft. Pilots are trained to fly even faster jets, prior to training on an Operational Conversion Unit.

Prince William's old digs?

RAF Valley is also home to two Search and Rescue lodger units as well as having two commercial flights between Valley and Cardiff International Airport. This is only so lazy AMs from north Wales don't have to drive the A470 from Cardiff Bay back to their homes up north though. It costs the taxpayer around £1.2 million a year and the planes run mostly empty.

I'm disappointed no one has arrested me yet so I cycle on a bit and take some more photos. Again, I wish I had my better camera with me rather than my cheap underwater Canon D30, perhaps a zoom lens would attract more interest? A super-fit female jogger passes me, I smile, but she ignores me. Should have sewn four gold stripes onto my panniers. No respect these days.

Has everyone left for the weekend or something? The place is ghostly quiet. Then I remember that Prince William no longer lives here, he's back in his palace somewhere, ah, that's where the SAS are! OK, let's get back on the bike.

I cycle down some more lanes then finally see a long stretch of road that looks promising. I cross the causeway (known locally as 'The Cobb') on a cycle lane of the busy A5 then detour to Penrhos Nature Reserve before finally rocking up in Holyhead, my furthest point west on my circuit of the Principality.

I see a road sign, take a photo then slowly make my way to town. Despite being the largest town in the county, Holyhead isn't actually on the main island, but on Holy Island.

Sun comes out right on cue!

I've made it. I stop on a park bench, take a photo of me pointing to where I am on the map and breathe a sigh of relief rather than jump in the air, fist punching in a gesture of achievement. To be honest I'm thinking of all the lanes I'm going to meet going back and wonder was it worth it?

The town is built around St Cybi's Church, which is built inside a rare, three-walled Roman fort (the fourth boundary being the sea, which used to come up to the fort). The current lighthouse is on South Stack on the other side of Holyhead Mountain but I don't cycle that far.

I've made it to Holy Island and that's enough for me. If I'd had another few days I would have probably stayed the night in Holyhead and had a few beers but instead I chill out in the sun for a bit.

I manage to squeeze in a quick sandwich and soon I'm contemplating the second half of my Welsh odyssey that is now all ahead of me. I relax for twenty minutes or so but soon I'm itching to get going again. The journey back will be a fair bit longer if I take the Route 5 that I'd planned so I decide to head off.

It's not long before I'm lost and right on cue my iPhone beeps. Mark is texting from Pontypridd. I think he's feeling guilty that he's abandoned me to my fate up north so feels the need to give me moral support from 200 miles away.

Somehow I've missed the turning for the Route 5 so I figure I might as well blast a few miles down the busy A5 before picking it up further on. I make my way back to the main road and immediately regret it, as the traffic is pretty bad.

I consult Google Maps again and decide I'll detour to Llangefni. I've never been there before, it's a big town by Ynys Môn standards and maybe I'll feel like a swift half seeing as the sun has come out now.

I find the town easy enough but can't find a pub with a beer garden so sit on a bench by the clock tower and finish my snacks.

Llangefni

I try to get back on the blue Sustrans route but there is some sort of fayre being set up in town with fences and security everywhere and the route is blocked. I try the B roads instead.

I cycle uphill out of town heading for Penmynydd. My Welsh isn't great but I decide this must be the head (or top) of the mountain so figure when I get there I'll have a fine view of the island and maybe see something other than lanes.

Henry Tudor's grandfather, Owen Tudor, came from Penmynydd but I never did make it as half way up the hill there was a big yellow sign that read 'Road Closed'. I enjoyed the ride back downhill into town feeling like I was in a remake of Groundhog Day. The cycle trail is blocked, the pubs are rubbish and the road is closed. Was I hear to stay I wondered?

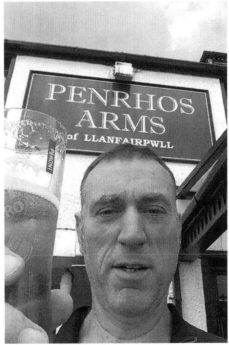

Lager, lager, lager!

No, don't panic I told myself. Sir John 'Kyffin' Williams, who was born in Llangefni, managed to escape so I'm sure I could too. The Welsh landscape painter lived at Llanfair PG and was one of the greatest painters of the

20th Century. I cycled out of town the same way I'd come in, up a hill and back to the A5, now a welcoming sight after my failure at orienteering my way through Llangefni.

As I've wasted an hour I decide to stay on the main road for a few miles and try to find either Route 5 or Route 8 to finish my day off on the island before crossing the sea again.

The journey back is much quicker though and I'm soon seeing signs for Llanfair PG again. I stop to take a photo of the bridge in the distance then decide to just push on and find a pub.

I stop at the Penrhos Arms and grab a beer. I tell the barman about the traffic and he informs me it's the Anglesey show, that's why it's so busy. Otherwise I'd have had the roads to myself.

I sit on a chair outside the pub and check my texts. Simon, from footie, who has been asking me how my training was going every week since I told the boys I was doing this ride, has sent me one. My usual answer is to state that I'll train on the ride. Why stress before eh? Mark has sent a few jokes (he's definitely feeling guilty, lol). I realise I'm not too far from the bridge now and then it'll be only a few miles to Bangor to find the guest house Sue has found for me.

I cross the bridge again and I'm back on mainland Wales. It feels slightly reassuring and I've decided to have a few beers tonight, after a good number of miles on Ynys Môn and hopefully a much easier day Saturday.

Bangor Cathedral

I'm back on a busy road as I hit the city centre and I'm surprised just how big a city Bangor is. I see the University up on the hill and head for the coast and Y Garth guest house run by ex-professional boxer Les Davies.

We have a chat and as well as telling me he was Welsh champion Les also informs me that he fought at the old Town Hall in Pontypridd. What a small world! He also shows me a photo of him with Muhammad Ali.

I pay Les for the room, then I shower and do the usual hanging up of sweaty clothes in front of open windows and hit the town! I'm starving as usual and fancy a beer.

I'd never been to Bangor before and my mate Aled (who has to work up here with the BBC) often tells me it's nothing to get excited about. I didn't believe him of course as it's got a cathedral and a great University. I was even thinking of studying marine biology here back in the mid-80s. I only changed my mind because I couldn't swim very far.

Well, Aled was right about the lanes and he was right about Bangor. I walked through the town and after literally five minutes I sent Aled a text. I then copied and pasted it to send to a few other mates when a text from Warren dropped in.

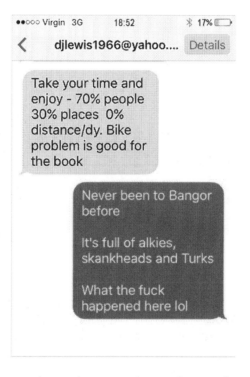

Warren is a true poet warrior and probably a repressed Buddhist. He was trying to keep me on track mentally by reminding me why we do these things. The people, the places, and in my case the wonder of the natural world too.

I knew Warren would know I'd understood his message so I copied and pasted my thoughts on Bangor to him too. The city centre was like a cross between Merthyr and City Road, Cardiff. Bangor is actually one of the smallest of the six cities in Wales though.

I found a trendy pub with giggling girls (possibly students) having a meal. I opted for the pub opposite. The Albion was a bit rough and a group of local alcoholic druggies looked like they were just about to kick off big time but after a bit of abuse from the barmaid they soon quietened down. It was like a north Wales 'Wonky bar'! Really funny.

Two meals for one

I asked the locals for a chip shop and got directed back the way I'd just walked. I decided to walk down the hill and treat myself to a sit down meal in The Castle pub. I asked for fish but they didn't have any batter. Then Sue phoned so I skipped the drink too and walked further down to the Old Glan pub instead.

I had another pint and ordered two meals for £8.99 - I had two massive cod, two portions of chips and two portions of beans that arrived on these huge plates – I scoffed the lot, desperate to make up for my calorie deficit.

137

I left and went for a walk around the longest high street in the UK, feeling a bit sick now. It must have been the beer. I wandered through a relative ghost town and took a few urban decay type photos. The place was a real shock to the system. A bit like Pontypridd, just more empty properties, kebab shops, takeaways etc.

I walked to the Garth Pier, the second longest in Wales at 1,500 feet long and looked for the blue cycle trail signs for the morning. I couldn't find any that looked promising but it was getting dark now so I went home, desperate to avoid the vampires and zombies I'd convinced myself were lurking under the pavement.

Bangor pier

Cycling Stats

Start: 6:30am
Distance: 64.23 miles
Total Distance: 401.65 miles
Average Speed: 10.27mph
Fastest Speed: 29.43mph
Cycling Time: 6 hrs 15 mins
Finish: 6:00pm
Calories: 4007
Ascent: 3681 ft
Descent: 3665 ft
Beers: 3

Route

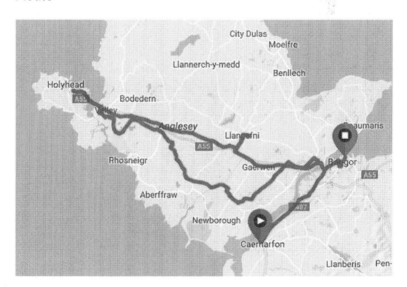

Hill Profile

 Day 9

Bangor to Prestatyn
Saturday 6th August 2016

iPhone alarm: Cathedral – Robyn Hitchcock

Woke up to seagulls screeching outside the window again. I wish I could remember to close them the night before. I have a slight hangover this morning, which just goes to show what a great athlete I'm becoming if all it takes is three pints to make me feel a bit muzzy.

Sunny at six o clock, it's almost like summer. Down for breakie and chat to Les again. He tells me about a time he did a charity walk from Bangor to Liverpool a few years back! Then he gives me £4 to go on the Just Giving page. As well as becoming Welsh welterweight champion Les also turned professional. It would have been nice to stay and chat but I had to get going, even though I had a relatively easy day ahead.

I cycle towards the pier and find the Sustrans signs pointing uphill and out of town. Then they take me down a dead end to a shipyard and then under a railway bridge and south towards Tregarth, which is definitely the wrong way so I turn around and come back. Got lost twice in three miles! Bit confused by all this and as there's no obvious route going the way I want to go I jump onto the A5 and head east. At least I know it's in the right general direction.

I find a trail / country lane that looks promising but then the 'Roman road' seems to go the wrong way – lost again! Who said this was going to be an easy day?

Go back to the main road and think, what the hell, I'll just take this a couple of miles until I see the Route 5 signs again, how hard can that be?

'Oh dear.'

I manage five miles of hard shoulder on the A55 North Wales Expressway, manage to find different swear words for buses, cars, vans, landies, tractors, milk floats, all trying to break the world land speed record. I half expect to see Jason Statham hurtling towards me in Frankenstein's Monster, a 2006 Ford Mustang GT A80 armed with 2 M134s, smokescreen, napalm and oil slick for defence, as well as a 6-inch-thick detachable steel plate on the rear called 'The Tombstone'. It's like being in a remake of Death Race 2000. Give me the A470 any day!

Nice scenery

Anyway, I didn't see Seren's mate Jason, but then my trouble really starts as the hard shoulder runs out. It's just me and an unstable bike and a grass verge. I push for a few hundred yards, try to find a way off the road but nothing is showing on my Google Maps app. Then I see a sign for Conwy – thirteen miles, unlucky for some.

'Bloody hell I've got to push through grass for four hours! This can't be right!'

I try *Evil Google* again, no luck.

Nothing for it, I push for another three or four miles until I see a turn off for Abergwyngregyn. I don't care if it's a farm track back to Bangor, I'm happy to be away from the long road to hell. I stop and ask this nice young couple for directions. Luckily they're locals and point me towards a railway bridge.

I find the bridge, ride under and turn left and as if by magic Mr Benn appears. Well actually he doesn't, but Route 5 does.

I curse my luck as well as my terrible map reading skills (where is Derek when you need a geographer?) and smile again. I suppose if it wasn't for these little trials and tribulations you'd never find out such interesting facts as Llanfairfechan is twinned with Pleumeleuc.

I cycle on and look across the water at yesterday's land of lanes. I start to hum a little jingle to myself. 'Say goodbye to Ynys Môn' to the tune of Billy Joel.

Great Orme

It's really sunny now as I find the lovely seafront trail, which according to the maps goes all the way to my final destination today, Prestatyn. In the distance is the unmistakeable shape of Llandudno and the Great Orme that gives me a real target to aim for as I pedal along at a good pace now.

After the French Revolution (1788-89) put paid to rich travellers doing their 'Grand Tour' of Europe, Wales suddenly became vogue with the idle rich. Artists and poets waxed lyrical about the beauty of our forgotten backwater, and the upper classes, keen to avoid their heads being lopped off on the continent looked closer to home for their gap years. North Wales in particular grew as a tourist destination. I got to thinking that maybe it's about time cyclists revived this tradition? I hope so!

I pause for a moment and look back the way I've come. A habit I find most rewarding, particularly as a photographer, as most of us only see what's right in front of us. What greets me is a weird and wonderful landscape.

Old quarries

The quarry at Penmaenmawr has existed since Neolithic times. Axe-heads and other tools, made from its distinctive stone have been found all over the British Isles. This ancient quarry was also used in the 1830's. In those days Penmaenmawr stone was carried by tramway to the seashore, and then by ship to Liverpool and other major ports. After the railway came to town in the 1840's the shipping trade collapsed but even today the quarry continues to thrive. The stone is universally popular for rail ballast, road building and the making of concrete. The Mersey Tunnel and the Hamburg By-Pass in Germany both use its stone.

Penmaenmawr was regarded as the producer of the hardest granite in the land. Labour came from all over the UK to work here, the village grew and so did the visitors, staying in local hostelries and turning the area from a small fishing and farming village into a popular seaside holiday resort.

Although those heady days are gone now the mountain and moorland behind still attracts many walkers. At the foot of the mountain, the expressway runs and the cycle trail runs parallel to it.

Skate park

I stop for a drink and snack at a skate park and admire the skill of a lad that looks older than me! I push on again, past the golf club and decide to stop for a rest at some ordinary-looking marina. I coast in and notice signs everywhere that say 'No bikes allowed to be leaned against pillars'. Bit weird I thought? Don't they want me to pop into the local store and buy a sandwich? I pop into the local store to buy a sandwich... Yep, I was right, they don't want my custom, bloody £3 for a flimsy sandwich on cardboard white bread! Bugger this for a game of soldiers, I jump back on the bike and leave the miserable old gits to it.

I'm really enjoying the trail now and head on to Conwy and its famous castle. Conwy Castle and the town walls were built by, guess who... Yes, well done, Edward I, between 1283 and 1289. It's getting boring now Teddy baby.

The oldest structure in town though is part of the town walls where one wall and the tower of Llywelyn the Great's Llys (court house) has been incorporated into the wall. Built on a rocky outcrop, with an apsidal tower, it is a classic, native Welsh build and stands out due to the presence of four window openings. It dates from the early 13th Century and is the most complete remnant of any of his Llys.

Unfriendly marina

I make it to the castle and stop to use the toilets. I follow the signs that direct me in a circle around the castle walls. I'm back where I started and still no toilets? Confused somewhat I stop at the RNLI and start chatting to a couple of very friendly locals.

'Any idea where the toilets are?' I ask.

'Yeh, they're down by there,' one chap helpfully points out.

I'm just about to do another lap of the town walls when the guy with him says 'No, they're shut mun, this council is crap.'

'Ah, that explains it.'

'Where you cycling to then?'

'Prestatyn. I started in Bangor this morning,' I reply.

'For charity?'

'Yeh, Prostate Cancer UK.'

'You can use our toilet then, up the stairs, don't mind the cleaner.'

I then get directions around the Great Orme and warned about the sand on the trail.

Conwy Castle

I cycle across the bridge to Llandudno Junction. I didn't realise it was so close to Conwy. Then I follow the cycle route all along the coast, looking back across the bay I get a much better view of the castle and the town nestled tight into the bay. It's an impressive scene and must have been quite scary for any bandits approaching from the sea.

I pedal past the second golf course of the day and then I hit the sand. I have to get off and push for a few metres, then back on, then back off, then back on...

I get stuck behind some mothers with prams who have no intention of letting me pass so just practice my balancing act for *Britain's Got Talent* on the hybrid Dawes as I average two or three miles per hour behind them. Then I see the cable car up above so cut across, following the trail signs into town.

Llandudno has been around since Stone Age times. It grew slowly as a settlement through the Bronze Age and then the Iron Age. The limestone headland is known to

146

seafarers as the Great Orme, which is Viking for sea serpent and is 679 feet high.

Although the area is only two miles long by one mile wide it is a SSSI and a Special Area of Conservation with a resident warden. Peregrine falcons, wild cotoneasters, cormorants, shags, guillemots, razorbills, puffins, kittiwakes and fulmars all nest here.

The headland is also famous for having a herd of about 200 Kashmir goats that have roamed here since the 19th Century.

Queen of Hearts

The Royal Welsh Regiment is permitted by the British monarch to choose an animal from the herd to be a Regimental Goat (if it passes selection, it is given the honorary rank of lance corporal). A rank that most infantrymen fail to reach, which to me says a lot about the out-dated traditions in our armed forces.

'Right son, run at that tank will you?'

'What?'

'Yep, the goat has given you a direct order.'

I cruise through town and pass one of the many Alice in Wonderland statues. There is a trail around the town, which commemorates the visit of Alice Liddell in 1861. Lewis Carroll's sequel *Through the Looking Glass* includes 'The Walrus' and 'The Carpenter' that are both big rocks from the town's west shore and some say that much of the town was featured in the drug-crazed, sex-mad, dreamscape children's book. Personally, I thought it was just about him trying to teach her maths?

Anyway, I'd run out of purple pills so I cycled on to the longest pier in Wales (at 2,295 feet), which was voted 'Pier of the Year 2005' by the members of the National Piers Society. I giggled to myself as I thought of *Have I Got News For You* discovering this publication. Then I saw that it was bursting to overflowing with Chinese tourists so cruised on past thousands, and I do mean thousands, of people, all congregating around a tiny bit of sand. It was a nice day, the sun was out but I did wonder why people do this. Some visitors had chips or ice creams in their hands. Massive invitation to the vicious seagulls and in a few short minutes I witnessed several attacks. It was like a walk down a Venezuelan barrio side street. OK, slight exaggeration, I actually love Herring Gulls and Lesser Black-backed Gulls – awesome birds that get a bad press.

Teeming hordes!

It's not long before I've seen enough. I felt weird entering this crowded seascape after being on my own for so long. I cycled up a big hill out of town and looked back at

148

the great views of the bay and pier below me in the distance.

I sped downhill and stopped at a Co-op for the usual meal deal thingie of sandwiches, a snack and a high sugar drink. I filled my panniers up with my booty and pedalled on to find the coast road again.

Flat coastal trail

I reach Rhos on Sea and sit on a bench to fill my stomach with calories. I look out to sea at the huge, offshore, Gwynt y Môr wind turbine farm. Its 576-megawatt capability is the second largest operating offshore wind farm in the world. There are 160 wind turbines that stand 490 feet above mean sea level.

The interesting bit for me though is that, as with all offshore wind farms in the UK, the Crown Estate owns the seabed. This means that any revenue goes to the Treasury. This wasn't always the case of course but in 1760 'mad' George III (who'd just lost America) decided to give the Crown Estate to the government 'cos it was too much hassle trying to keep track of all that cash. The monarchs then got their money for nothing from the civil list, which still exits today of course. These days the UK government gets about £12 billion worth of assets from the Crown Estate.

Anyway, the wind farms are leased and run mostly by npower, a German company. And we wonder why our energy bills are so high! I wonder how high they'll be when the Tories let the Chinese take over our nuclear power stations for a few backhanders.

Sandwiches over I cycle on to Colwyn Bay, famous for being the birthplace of the worst James Bond ever – Timothy Dalton, and Monty Python legend Terry Jones.

It's a lovely ride along the north Wales coast, the sun is warm and there is a nice cool breeze. The only real problem I encounter is the way people who walk, cycle and push prams still haven't worked out the bloody keep-left rule!

I stop to take some photos of the dilapidated pier for my *urban decay* series.

Colwyn Bay Pier

I cycle through Abergele. I don't stop 'cos it isn't very nice. Then I eventually reach Rhyl.

Rhyl used to be a popular holiday destination but an influx of Scousers and Mancs after the war saw the place change quite drastically. Famous people from the town are murderess Ruth Ellis (the last woman hanged in UK), Peter Moore (serial killer) and Albert Gubay who founded Kwik Save. The town also ranked highly in *Crap Towns*.

The town has recently gone more upmarket though with millions of pounds of Welsh Government investment to the seafront and town, which will probably result in a decline in the fortunes of Prestatyn, a bit further along.

I stop for a quick rest and chat to a lovely lady from St Asaph, out for a day's cycling, and she takes a photo of me in front of a big red thing.

Red Rhyl

I look around for a bit and take some more photos but eventually I decide it's time to finish the day's ride, a lovely, relaxing day after a nightmare start in Bangor, and I push on to my final port of call – Prestatyn.

I reach the town, and stop to admire the silvery statue and Offa's Dyke signpost, which I hope to reach on foot, in a few years time, when me and my daughter Eve eventually make it this far. We started our walk of the path at Chepstow a couple of summer's ago and have made it to Llanthony Priory so far.

I leave the beach behind and slowly cruise up the High Street trying to remember the last time I was here. It was actually about twenty years ago when me and Mark cycled the length of Wales (Prestatyn to Pontypridd). I remember we stayed at a little B&B and at breakfast we had the owner bring in a small cake, as it was Mark's birthday. Why she was singing 'Happy Birthday to Mike' we had no idea though.

I looked around town as I cycled but couldn't make out any of the old prehistoric settlements or the Roman influence. Somebody from Rhyl must have moved them?

Prestatyn

I reach my digs for the night, the overpriced Halcyon Quest guest house which I found on the terrible *booking.com* website. I check-in and ask where I can securely lock my bike up as I requested when I booked the room.

'Nowhere really,' says the nice young chap, doing his best but still not being much help.

'OK, I'll take it up to the room,' I reply.

'Oh, well you could put it in that shed out the back,' he remembers.

I do, but am not pleased that it doesn't even have a lock on it! I lock my frame to a beer barrel and hope I'm up before the drayman calls.

'Would you like breakfast?' asks the helpful lad.

'Oh yes please,' I say, eager to fill out the form pushed my way.

I tick everything that is edible and also add to the form under the section that says 'If you'd like an earlier breakfast just ask' 'I'd like breakfast by 7:00am please'. I also make a point of asking for an early breakie as I have a long day ahead tomorrow and don't really trust this lad's ability to read and follow simple instructions.

'Can't do seven o'clock,' the guy says.

'Oh. OK, how about half past seven then?' I ask.

'No, eight thirty.'

'But it says here I can ask for an earlier breakfast?'

'Yeh, I know, but no-one will be in on the weekend.'

'Ah, so eight thirty then?'

'Oh. Do you still want breakfast?' he asks, hoping to save some bacon and egg for himself no doubt.

'Yes, I bloody do!' I raise my voice, throwing the form back at him.

'OK.'

'T@%t!' almost under my breath.

Then I inspect the room. I feel like I'm in one of those crappy, reality TV shows where they go to other people's hotels and moan about finding a pube in the bosh.

No shampoo. Luckily I acquired some from my previous haunts. I had a shower and a quick relax on the bed with a chocolate bar. Uncomfy mattress, springs coming through and digging in my dodgy back – great! I head to town for a beer.

I find a chippy and stock up my glycogen stores on chips, curry, pie and some battered thing. Then I pop in to Archies bar for a pint. It's a pretty sterile chain pub so I sit outside in the slightly raised beer terrace overlooking the main road.

Had a laugh listening to this idiot of a local who really fancied himself. He was originally from Manchester he told me. There were a group of local girls on the next table to him who seemed to be ignoring his antics so he got up, dropped his pants and showed them his genitalia. Luckily he was facing away from me so I didn't get a close-up and just had to rely on the giggles from the girls to judge the size (or lack of) and general appearance of his equipment. Not that I was that interested of course.

I wasn't sure if this was normal Prestatyn behaviour or whether he'd been parachuted in from the rival Rhyl Tourist Board so decided not to follow suit in case I'd just happened upon the only bar in town where this was considered acceptable behaviour.

Then I got to thinking. Maybe he'd stayed at my room yesterday? That would explain the pubic hair in the bathroom.

As I was sipping my beer and chuckling to myself Mark rang.

'Where are you?' he asked.

'In Prestatyn, watching a bloke show his meat and two veg to some local lasses.'

'Duw, duw, you find all the classy joints don't you,' replied Mark.

I finished my £2.90 pint of Carlsberg (which was quite reasonable) and decided I'd had enough of his merry banter and took my leave. I had a bumpy bed to lie in.

I got back to the guest house and retired to watch some rugby on the TV. I'd forgotten it was the Olympics and the women were playing sevens. I had another Cadburys Wispa and listened to the awful karaoke coming from the bar below. So much for an early night, wait until I get on Trip Advisor I thought.

Cycling Stats

Start: 8:30am
Distance: 43.77 miles
Total Distance: 445.42 miles
Average Speed: 9.71mph
Fastest Speed: 28.97mph
Cycling Time: 4 hrs 30 mins
Finish: 5:00pm
Calories: 2563
Ascent: 2218 ft
Descent: 2093 ft
Beers: 1

Route

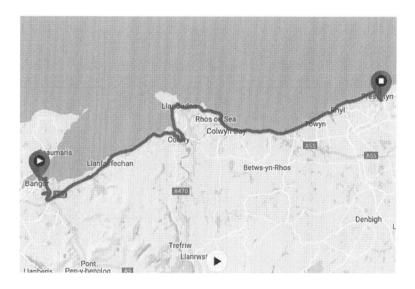

Hill Profile

 Day 10

Prestatyn to Oswestry
Sunday 7th August 2016

iPhone alarm: The High Road – Broken Bells

I didn't have any Mike Peters or The Alarm on my iTunes so I settled for homage to yesterday's beautiful bike trail instead. The high road would be my lasting memory of the north Wales coastline, as opposed to some bloke's old boy.

I rise early, looking forward to my sausages. I know I have a long day ahead and also have no idea where I'm going apart from heading south. There doesn't seem to be many Sustrans routes in this part of the world after I leave the coast.

What I really need is a big greasy breakie like you'd get at a truck stop, the old Roath diner or the Albion Kebab House, Cilfynydd. Then I remember the eight thirty start.

'Bugger.'

I'm awake at six o'clock but can't have breakie for another two and a half hours. I decide to watch some TV, listen to some music, pack, re-pack, get the bike ready by eight and maybe grab some orange juice and cereal. They probably put that out the night before.

I try the door to the stairs. It's locked, has an alarm and is probably on a timer. I wander around the upstairs of the pub like Jack Torrance until I find a staircase. I go down and find myself outside in the car park. I look in through the windows and it's like the Mary Celeste. I meet a Scottish couple that also can't get in so decide to head off up the road rather than risk food poisoning.

'Bugger. Forty quid and no breakie, bugger, I hate losing food.'

I decide to cycle fast and get a few miles under my shorts by eight thirty, that way I can imagine being back in the pub and way behind schedule.

It's a beautiful morning, quite cold, but the coastline is very dramatic. I take a photo about five miles out of town and hope that the huge, dark cloud is heading towards England rather than following me east, then south down to the border. I'm still cycling on the trail though and make great progress.

Forbidding cloud

I pass Mostyn and the infamous Duke of Lancaster Fun Ship car boot sale. Boy I know how to live it up on a Sunday morning in north Wales!

I toy with the idea of continuing down to the industrial Deeside area, to the site of past coal mining, ship building, steel, railway, brickworks and so on, but knowing me I'll want to carry on to Chester Zoo so stop when I reach the town of Flint instead.

Flint is interesting because it has the oldest town charter in Wales, around 1284. This meant that the people of the town had certain rights under the old feudal system as opposed to the serfs living in villages that could still be killed for not wiping their nose on a Wednesday. Happy days and ones the present government would love to see us return to.

Flint Castle was the first of Edward Longshanks iron ring to be built but I didn't visit as I was all 'castled-out' to be honest! And there were more to come, later on in the day too.

Today most residents speak English as opposed to Welsh, with Polish also heard everywhere thanks to the EU's free movement policy. Famous people from Flint include Ian Rush, ex-Welsh football captain and Jade Jones, double Olympic champion in Taekwondo.

Apparently a distant relative of Tom 'I'm not gay' Cruise came from Flint but we won't mention that in case his scientology friends sue us for mentioning Xenu, the dictator of the Galactic Confederacy, who 75 million years ago brought billions of people to Earth in DC-8-like spaceships, then chucked them out next to volcanoes before blowing them up with hydrogen bombs. But like I say, we won't mention this.

The trail takes me uphill. I'm starting to feel really chilly in the wind now so stop at a Gulf petrol station for a rip off £2:20 vanilla latte from the American machine in the corner.

I joke to the attendant that they should have chairs for me to sit down and drink my hot, sugary beverage. The lovely Sue is just finishing her shift.

'You want a chair do you love?'

'Oh yes please,' I reply with a grin.

'Oh, and how about a nice massage as well?' she offers.

I turn around and the next thing I know these magic hands are kneading the tight muscles of my knackered neck. I'm just about to say 'lower' when she stops. Ah well, can't have everything, but certainly can't fault these north Welsh ladies!

I pedal on up Flint mountain and am pleasantly reintroduced to Welsh hills, something you forget for a while along the north coast. I stuff a few energy bars down my throat, eat a packet of salty crisps and a sandwich then speed off to look for more food.

I make great time to Wrecsam using the main road as I've lost the trails somehow. It's a big town but a bland, carbon copy of most other high streets in the UK these days.

It wasn't always like this of course. In Mesolithic times (8,000 BC) the town looked much nicer. Even during the Bronze Age there was more going on, especially in the metalwork industry. After the Romans left though law and order went right out the window. Saxons invaded, pushing the Celts out, then Vikings came and finally the Normans.

Colourful sheep

The Marcher lords administered the town in the late 13th Century and Wrecsam became quite prosperous. In fact by 1391 it was wealthy enough for a bard, jester, juggler, dancer and goldsmith to earn a living there. Maybe the guy from Archies pub in Prestatyn could get a job here I thought?

He could certainly get a drink here, if he visited, because the Wrexham Brewery was the first to produce lager anywhere in the UK when German immigrants came to town in 1882.

159

I stop for a drink at the beautiful St Giles church, take a photo, and then spot a colourful sheep in the grounds. And I thought scientology nutters were weird? Well it is a Sunday so I suppose it's allowed.

Out of Wrecsam I head for Ruabon. Mainly 'cos it has a nice sounding name, I've never been there before and it looks like there are some cycle lanes. Unfortunately though it turns out to be just those 'highly protective' white lines painted on a road that is clogged full with heavily congested traffic. You know the sort of traffic. The kind that completely ignores a cyclist and pretends to themselves that if they close their eyes as they pass and go fast enough and near enough that nothing will happen. I invent a new swear word.

From Ruabon I head inland to Llangollen on cycle paths but turn down to Pontcysyllte Aqueduct, the most poorly signposted tourist attraction in the world for people on bikes. Although I have to say, once you find it, it's absolutely brilliant.

Canal barges

Pontcysyllte Aqueduct and canal consists of a continuous group of civil engineering features dating from the British Industrial Revolution and is a World Heritage site like Blaenavon and the castles of Wales.

160

The canal brought produce from the English lowlands to the rugged Welsh landscape and the bridges that were built to achieve this are a testament to the remarkable engineering of two of the UK's greatest heroes.

The aqueduct was built between 1795 and 1808 by Thomas Telford and William Jessop and is today one of Wales' best tourist sites.

Pontcysyllte Aqueduct

Pontcysyllte Aqueduct crosses the Dee Valley on nineteen cast iron spans at a height of 126 feet. An awesome structure, internationally recognised as an absolute masterpiece of waterways engineering and a pioneering example of iron construction. The structure is over 1,000 feet long but only 12 feet wide.

The canal highlights the new developments in British engineering that occurred during the Industrial

Revolution that were subsequently adopted throughout the whole Empire.

Although the river is now used for tourists on boating trips and there is a café and gift shop the area certainly hasn't been ruined. In fact it's very pleasant and I even took my top off for a spot of impromptu Vitamin D while I ate my sandwiches.

It has been in continuous use for over two hundred years and not wanting to put a spanner in that record I decided it only fair to cycle across myself. Unfortunately, although the cycle trail route does indeed cross the valley there were just too many people on the aqueduct for me to saddle up so I just had to push my Dawes over.

I paused halfway for a look down, felt a bit dizzy (I'm not great with heights), took some photos then nearly fell in the water. I managed to regain my balance and pushed on.

At the other end the cycle trail continues along the canal towpath. This is great, flat pedalling, with just a few picnics, dogs and lost tourists to avoid.

I carried on through the Whitehouse Tunnel, which was dark but fun at 570 feet long. Then I carried on the trail until the next tunnel and praised my iPhone and new phone contract for giving me Google Maps and some data allowance. Without this I'd still be cycling and would have ended up in the Irish Sea or something but exiting the canal (no signposts anywhere) I got to the road and saw a load of cars heading up a lane.

'That must be the castle,' I said out loud to no one in particular.

I'm feeling good, the weather is great, and I'm in holiday mode and enjoying the scenery. I decide to cycle up to Chirk Castle. It can't be far I tell myself.

It isn't. It is uphill though. I hate hills.

I climb to the top without stopping, mainly 'cos there's loads of tourists, scouts, cars, knights with lances and kids looking at me as I struggle to find a low enough gear. I make it OK though. The view is great and it's well worth the climb for the castle as well.

The castle was built in 1295 by Roger Mortimer de Chirk and stayed in posh people's hands until just a few years back. Sir Thomas Myddleton, a founder of the East India Company, bought it in 1595 and it has been in the family's hands ever since. In 2004 though the current occupier, Guy Myddleton left because it was too noisy a place to bring up his kids, what with all the tourists visiting. Not sure what austerity-hit sink council estate he's moved his family to instead but I bet he misses the old place?

Chirk Castle

I enjoy the great downhill from the castle, then I'm out of Chirk and onto a B road. I cycle on, then bank a fast bend and I find myself in Shropshire (that's in England). Bit of a horrible A road next, then a trail up and down past some farms and into Oswestry.

I have a quick look around town and discover it's much like many other border towns, e.g. Ludlow, Welshpool, etc.

I use my iPhone and Google Maps again to find the digs Sue has booked for me. It's great when it works but I think I prefer asking people for directions rather than trying to steer my packhorse bike with one hand whilst constantly turning my mobile around to follow my little blue dot careering down the road. Probably not in the Health and Safety manual either.

I eventually manage to put the mobile the right way up and find Montrose Guest House, a beautiful old period house just south of town. I have a shower and hit the town.

I decide to go back on the real ale. I have a pint of Shropshire light ale in the Oak Inn. It's OK, bit weak though.

Oswestry

I find an Indian takeaway that seems to be doubling up as a chippy. I have curry and chips and fishcake once we overcome the language barrier, which takes a little while. Especially when she tries to explain the special offers they have. It's like trying to decide which BT broadband and calls package deal is the best. I go for the cheaper option and it turns out to cost exactly the same as the special offer where I got a sausage as well. Exactly like BT then in fact. I think of asking for that as well but not sure I'm up for more linguistic jousting just for a sausage.

Oswestry is a typical market town and the largest in Shropshire. It has one of the best Iron Age hill forts in Britain, probably built around 800 BC. Although I'm in England, just across the border I felt this was a necessary part of the trip, as a lap of Wales has to include the Welsh border country, otherwise I'd need a hovercraft not a bike.

During Saxon times, legend has it that Oswald of Northumbria, who was killed and chopped up in battle gave his name to the town because a raven flew off with his arm and dropped it in a tree where miracles subsequently happened. I have this strange feeling that Tom Cruise and John Travolta are going to appear any moment. Anyway, Oswald's Tree – Oswestry, get it? Sounds like a special offer at the chippy to me, no miracle there mind you.

Bloke with a sheep

Years later the Normans came of course and various battles meant the town changed nationalities as quickly as a politician changes his or her heartfelt, lifelong convictions. There are many Welsh names in town, Owain Glyndŵr visited in 1400 and nearly burnt the place to the ground and the castle was reduced to a pile of rocks in the English Civil War.

Oswestry is also famous as the birthplace of WWI poet Wilfred Owen, who wrote realistic war poetry on the horrors of the trenches and gas warfare rather than flowery rubbish like some of his contemporaries. His poem *Dulce et Decorum est* is known for its horrific imagery and condemnation of war.

I wander about for a bit but soon the cold forces me into another hostelry to warm up. I have a pint of Three Tuns real ale in The Bailey Head and wonder if any Mott the Hoople tribute bands are in town. They aren't.

I chat to the pub locals for a while, they are OK, but it's not a great pint to be honest. I think about having another somewhere else but then remember my promise to my kindly, old landlady that I wouldn't be late.

I'm home and tucked up in bed by 9:00pm. I have a great sleep for once, probably the best of the whole trip. Must stick to real ale from now on.

Cycling Stats

Start: 8:00am
Distance: 54.21 miles
Total Distance: 499.63 miles
Average Speed: 9.92mph
Fastest Speed: 28.30mph
Cycling Time: 5 hrs 28 mins
Finish: 6:00pm
Calories: 3562
Ascent: 3599 ft
Descent: 3291 ft
Beers: 2

Route

Hill Profile

Day 11

Oswestry to Knighton
Monday 8ᵗʰ August 2016

iPhone alarm: God Save the Queen – Sex Pistols

I pick an appropriate song to wake up to as I'm in England this morning. I hope it wasn't too loud for my little old lady. I hear someone stirring in the big, empty house so venture downstairs and grab some cereal from the box. Nice breakie from my eighty-two year old host. Never did get a name, just know that she likes to watch the swimming at the Olympics on the TV. I tidy up my dishes, retrieve my bike from the garage, say my goodbyes and get on the road, desperate to find a cycle trail.

Hay bales

I pedal south and soon find some nice rural vistas. It's also quite refreshing to find hay in bales as opposed to those all covered in plastic. I take a photo of what might soon become a thing of the past! I blame the Chinese. I blame them for everything. Ivory poaching, rhino slaughter, dog meat torture, the occupation of Tibet, jaguar hunting, loss of European manufacturing jobs, the rape of Africa's natural resources, any bad pint I ever have, the list goes on... then I start singing Jethro Tull songs in my head about the landscape and people's connection to it just as I cycle onto an A road. Oh dear, oh deary me.

What did I say about rush hour and avoiding it? Oops, I forgot. I now have two hours of dodging in and out of laybys and farm track entrances to avoid becoming roadkill. In between the roar of heavy vehicles I hear the constant accompaniment of buzzard calls, which helps to keep me going.

Border country

The first three and a half miles is like Le Mans for cement mixers, white van men and livestock lorries until I eventually find a narrow pavement. Not a good start to the day – Sustrans where are you? An Offa's Dyke cycle trail maybe?

I stick to the pavements until I reach the English / Welsh border. I take some photos to compare. I think the old enemy edges it with a pretty flower display whilst the Welsh side just emphasises motorbike crashes, the number of fatalities and police speed traps – happy days!

I might be on the busy A483 but I do pass some beautiful houses, which gets me thinking that estate agents must only arrange visits on a Sunday in this part of the world. Either that or each property must come with a free supply of ear protectors.

Corn circles

I continue to play 'Frogger' on the main road, constantly looking out for pavements or cycle tracks but it's a tricky one. I make full use of the Doppler effect to judge when to pull over and when to speed up.

Eventually though I turn off the highway to hell towards Shrewsbury at Buttington, just before Welshpool, with a sore butt, then over the bridge and first right towards Leighton on Route 81.

The roads are much easier now and I start to enjoy the scenery again. I turn left out of Forden then towards Chirbury and a great downhill where I pick up a fair bit of speed. The road rolls up and down as I head for Church Stoke passing in and out of Wales and England.

I pass up the opportunity to visit the ruins of Montgomery Castle, first built just after the Norman invasion and improved 150 years later but I see it in the distance and can appreciate the strategic position.

The town of Montgomery was where King Henry III granted Llywelyn ap Gruffudd the title Prince of Wales in 1267. Fifteen years later though, in December 1282, the army of Montgomery marched to Builth Wells to kill him. Real buggers these kings eh!

In 1402 the walled town of Montgomery was attacked by Owain Glyndŵr and burned. However, the stone castle fortress held out against the attack.

I'm making the route up as I go along now and then it occurs to me that I've seen no Sustrans blue signs for quite a while when I happen upon a Route 44 sign.

Zipped-up house

I leave Wales again and cross the border into England. I'm like a Frenchman living next door to a brothel. After a few miles I turn into Bishops Castle, stop to take some photos of the very cool, painted houses, then pedal uphill through the quaint little town to have some food.

Although typical of many border towns Bishops Castle has become a bit of an alternative community where artists, musicians, writers and craftspeople hang out. The surrounding area is popular with walkers and the Shropshire Way runs through the town. The ancient trackway of the Kerry Ridgeway, a prehistoric Bronze Age route, also runs from the town. There are also two microbreweries, including the Three Tuns, the UK's oldest brewery.

I chat to a nice shopkeeper, look for the castle ruins, by doing a lap of the small town but decide sandwiches in the sun are more important. I sit beneath the clock tower, top off and enjoy my Co-op Ploughman's triple-decker with crisps, Lucozade and more water.

Bishops Castle

Back on the bike I push on up a few hills against the wind, heading towards Clun Forest. It's a long climb up but worth it for the great views of the patchwork fields of the valley below. Once again the effort riding up is rewarded with a nice ride down into the small town of Clun, home of the Green Man festival.

I start singing Tull's *Jack in the Green* to myself as I ponder the origins of this weird pagan symbol. A Green Man is basically a face surrounded by or made from

172

leaves. Many carvings and sculptures occur on churches throughout the UK but similar symbolism has been recorded in many different cultures all over the world, which points to either an independent evolution or alien visitors. Shit, maybe Tom Cruise and his spaceships have been here before?

Anyway, as I whizz into town I'm greeted by masses of local people shouting, cheering and waving. I'm completely underwhelmed by the welcome. They've even put a large banner up for me! I don't have the heart to tell them I'm staying in Knighton.

Clun

I stop for a quick half of real ale, outside the White Horse Inn and enjoy the hot sun. I contemplate the mythology surrounding the Green Man, think about how this trip has resulted in a rebirth of sorts for myself. I hadn't really been on a road bike for eleven years before this trip, apart from two quick training rides. Then my bike problems, then the rebirth of the Dawes. Yeh, it was all making sense now. Apart from the giant zipper on the house.

I enjoy my beer and have some time before Knighton so try to visit Clun Castle. I say tried because I didn't actually see it. It's not very bike friendly and after trudging through a field I gave up and went back to my bike. What the hell, it's not exactly Caerphilly, Caernarfon or Pembroke so what more would I see? The playwright John Osborne was born near Clun but I don't *Look Back in Anger* I just jump back in the saddle and pedal off.

After a few minutes I change my mind. The bloody hills out of Clun are pretty big, up and down, but I guess worth it for the great views of the valley.

I cycle on for a bit, pass the train station and suddenly I'm back in Wales. I stop for a pint of Butty Bach, a much-needed refreshment at the Horse and Jockey pub and chat to the locals inside, some of whom are Welsh, some of who are English. Not sure about the sheepdog, he didn't say.

Knighton

I'd been to Knighton a few times before and it was good to be back. Right smack bang on a well preserved part of Offa's Dyke it's a lovely little town popular with hikers.

I sit in the beer garden and chat to two motorcyclists, the one lad is a huge Irish bloke who gives me the impression, with his imposing stature and his twenty questions, that he is an ex-SAS interrogator while his large mate is probably the sergeant major studying me from afar. Weird how I get these images?

174

Anyway, they jump back on their motorised versions of what I'm doing and whizz off to Scotland or somewhere in the late afternoon. I then talk to the table of locals I'm sat with, a ramblers group, about me writing up this cycling trip. The leader of the group asks me about my novels and I modestly tell him that they are the best crime thrillers you can ever read and are currently being turned into Hollywood blockbusters starring Clive Owen as Hal and Hayley Atwell as Jenny.

'Really?'

'No, I was kidding.'

I feel quite at home here in the sun and fancy a few more beers but instead decide to phone Don, who my wife said 'he's really nice and will pick you up if you're too tired to cycle to his place'. Apparently I'm staying at Don's B&B tonight.

Knighton is yet another border town, it has an old Iron Age hill fort, got attacked by good old Owain in 1402 and also has a clock tower, like many others in the UK. It also has the River Teme running through town, which we all know is one of the best fishing rivers in Britain. I only know this 'cos Derek told me eleven years ago.

I'm thinking of a third beer when a van pulls up.

'Hi, Dave, I'm Don, are you ready?'

'Yep, good to meet you, can I buy you a beer?'

We put the bike in the back of the van and Don drives, at about 80mph, along three miles of country lanes to his house. It's a bit like going for a run with Gerald Davies or Shane Williams. I think we arrive before we leave!

Sue has hit the jackpot this time with her accommodation foray of mid Wales. Don and Kath Szmidt run The Mill, at Lloyney, right opposite the pub and have turned the old place into a fantastic hideaway. The décor and atmosphere are wonderful, as you'd expect from an ex-Art teacher. Don is also a keen cyclist who runs trips for anyone interested.

I shower and change and pop over the Lloyney Inn for some fish, chips and beans. Don joins me and we have two pints of nice real ale before heading back to his place for some whisky and a great chat about all the places we've both been to.

On my 'to do list' are the following countries: Cuba, Ethiopia, Malawi, Nepal and Namibia. Not the most obvious of holiday destinations for many people you might think. Don has just recently been to three of them! I'm well impressed.

Cycling Stats

Start: 8:15am
Distance: 43.83 miles
Total Distance: 543.46 miles
Average Speed: 10.16mph
Fastest Speed: 36.06mph
Cycling Time: 4 hrs 19 mins
Finish: 5:00pm
Calories: 3014
Ascent: 3284 ft
Descent: 3064 ft
Beers: 3½
Whisky: 1

Route

Hill Profile

 Day 12

Knighton to Abergavenny
Tuesday 9th August 2016

iPhone alarm: Wild Horses – The Rolling Stones

Up early despite a few beers yesterday. Good chat to Don again. Great breakie and then a brief discussion regards the route I should be taking. I ask about the hill out of Knighton straight down to Presteigne and Don's warning about 'killer' hill, persuades me to avoid that one! The route I choose was much longer but Don assures me it's far easier.

Outside the mill Don pumps my tyres up and cleans my chain of two weeks of mud, whilst shaking his head and tutting a lot. I just tell him Derek normally does this.

Hills and more hills

I set off and I'm happy with the idea of extra miles until I reach the town centre then pant my way up a 6% out of Knighton! This is a huge, long hill that just seems to go up and up forever. I curse my new mate Don and wonder if he's done this on purpose, then I look back at the alternative route and see pretty much hills everywhere.

I'm sweating already but eventually reach the top. Then it's a few miles downhill, which is great, followed by more of the same.

I seem to be heading west towards mid Wales now, and away from Hay Bluff in the distance but push on anyway. I climb another hill, go around Radnor forest and start to get cold with the sweat. I stop for a minute to put my waterproof on top of the two t-shirts I'm wearing.

On a good downhill a huge red kite swoops low in front of me and then it starts to drizzle. As the rain chills me again I'm hoping this is the last of the hills but no such luck, here's another one. I love the great Welsh, August weather, even though the forecast was sun of course! Benny!

I enjoy a nice downhill and turn left at Penybont, heading back east now and away from Llandrindod Wells. Finally the road gets easier as I join the main A44.

Chocolate snack

Lots of nice rolling road but I'm still sweating like a pig. I stop near the top of one hill for a snack and a selfie. I look back down the valley at where I've come from and it makes me feel much better. Then the sun comes out.

I cycle on and find the roads much flatter and faster now. I pop across the border into England again, this time to Herefordshire and soon I'm in the town of Kington.

Great views

I'm quite tired now and feel even worse when I see a sign telling me Knighton is only a few miles back yet I've cycled over twice that distance to avoid the big hills. Don obviously had no idea just how unfit I was. I think maybe I should have just pushed it up the 'killer' hill.

Kington is only two miles from Wales yet is on the western side of Offa's Dyke. The town has been English for over a thousand years though. It's a similar, small market town to Knighton – very confusing!

Interesting though is that Kington may have derived from King's-ton, being Anglo-Saxon for 'King's Town', whereas Presteigne would mean 'Priest's Town' and Knighton 'Knight's Town'. I can't find any Daveton on the map so figure it's back to the lottery if I ever want to buy a house around these parts.

Incidentally, songwriter Mike Oldfield, of Tubular Bells fame, lived nearby when he recorded Hergest Ridge, which is one of the highest points around at 1,400 feet. Nowhere near as high as the Welsh hills I'm heading towards though.

I don't loiter in Kington as I'm happy to be getting close to my dinnertime stop at Hay-on-Wye. I take a few quick photos then carry on. The Herefordshire countryside is most agreeable as I pass through the village of Eardisley then look out for the turning west towards the next pit stop come sandwich shop.

There are some nice fast stretches now although the road starts to get busier again. I push on and soon reach Whitney-on-Wye, which sits on the English side of the River Wye.

Toll Bridge Sign

During the Captain Swing riot movement of 1830, Whitney's dispossessed farm labourers protested against the introduction of new threshing machines and the loss of their livelihoods. They threatened arson in order to try to obtain a living wage. Funny enough Ed Milliband wanted the same thing more recently for the poorer workers of our country but no one voted for him.

I stop at Whitney on Wye to take some photos of the famous toll bridge, which charges cars but not poor Welsh cyclists. The 1780, Grade II listed building is just up from The Boat Inn, a nice pub with great food, right on the river. The toll bridge acts as a shortcut to Hay-on-Wye.

Whitney-on-Wye

I crossed the river on the rickety, old wooden bridge and cycled until I reached the Co-op for, yes you've guessed it, another meal deal. I stock up on sandwiches and cruise into the world famous, second-hand book town of Hay-on-Wye.

Hay is the National Book Town of Wales and hosts the annual Hay Festival, a major literary festival, and world famous with luvvies all over the world. Plenty of famous people have attended over the years including Bill Clinton who probably said something about his friend Monica not inhaling.

There are some nice pubs in the town, most famous is 'Rosie's' where Marianne Faithful, Neil Kinnock, and some of the Great Train Robbers have drank. I remember going in many years back with my mate Brian the alcoholic and only being allowed two pints of cider. There were

Woodbines for sale and a calendar from 1930-something on the wall. Then Rosie nearly burnt it down and had to give it up. It's now The Three Tuns, a posh food place unrecognisable from the good old days.

I cycle to the toilet but when I see the 20p charge to urinate in my own country I pedal on. I'll stick to hedgerows, or thinking about it maybe I'll do a Paula Radcliffe and use the pavement. They might put a blue plaque up when my novels sell – 'Famous Author Pissed Here'.

I stop at Richard Booth's second-hand bookshop and a nice Scottish tourist takes a photo of me. It was Richard who put Hay on the map when on 1 April 1977, he conceived a publicity stunt in which he declared Hay-on-Wye to be an 'independent kingdom' with himself as its monarch and his horse as Prime Minister.

Outside Booths

The book town has since thrived with a healthy tourist industry based on literary, arts and music events. I met him years ago, a couple of times, and we always chatted about books. I remember one time I was going on about African exploration and Richard took me into his little room where he had, locked away, some of his rarest books. He showed me original texts by Stanley and my hero Sir Richard Burton, the explorer. I was eager to look

183

until I enquired about the price, then I got rather nervous that I would damage the precious pages so gave them back. He was a nice guy.

Hay is also less well known as the place from which solicitor Herbert Rowse Armstrong, the 'Hay Poisoner', came from. He was hanged for murder in 1922. So always check your curry after a few beers in Hay.

Books, Hay Castle

I had no need of foreign muck though as I had my freshly prepared chicken salad sandwiches, prawn cocktail crisps and Lucozade to consume. The town was very busy as there was some sort of ridiculously overpriced, local produce market going on so I made my way to the castle for some peace and quiet and sat in the sun for ten minutes.

While I was lying there soaking up the rays a young yummy mummy lets her little boy run up to the castle to play. Listening to the conversation I can't help thinking she's being a little over protective, worrying about his safety in such a safe and pleasant town.

'Can I go up here mummy,' he shouts.
'OK then, but be careful.'
'I will mummy.'
Two minutes later I hear...

'Did you get him Ollie?'

It's then I realise that humanity is doomed. In a town with over a million books to read this little scamp is chasing bloody Pokémon's. It's time to go.

I saddle up, check my supplies of high-calorie energy bars and water then slowly cruise through a packed town. I pass the Swan At Hay (my favourite pub) and turn left at the bottom of the hill and see a Route 42 sign. I follow the little blue markers towards one of the biggest hills on my whole ride.

It's not a typo!

I find the forest road and pedal on. This is easy I say to myself. Then the road starts to get a little steeper. Still easy I'm saying. Then I see some local wit has written things on the tarmac. Things like 'Get ready', 'On your marks', 'Get set', that kind of thing.

I manage a few bends after the 'Go' but soon realise I'm in danger of breaking my chain, my lungs or my knees. Time to push, but don't tell Derek. Especially having just seen a really informative road sign.

It's a hell of a climb (or should that be push?) but no worse than the mountain behind Pontypridd on the way to Eglwysilan. I let a few tractors pass then stop for an energy bar. I manage to cycle a bit but mostly it's push for a bit, then ride for a bit.

When I get near the top though the views are stunning. I get back on after the 'Nearly there' road markings and look very professional to any passing cars who glance admiringly out the window at this Olympic athlete, in the peak of physical fitness, that they crawl past in their car's lowest gear. I force a smile at a few passengers and then stop to admire the views.

Watch out for Werewolves

It's a great hill that I'm sure Derek and Aled would love with their extra sprockets and I make a mental note to upgrade my chain set for the next ride I do, ten or eleven years from now.

I take some photos then cycle a bit further on only to want to stop again and take more photos. I have to say this is one of the best landscapes in Wales and certainly

186

one of the best sights I've seen on my trip so far. The weather is pretty good too.

In the distance I see Twmpa or Lord Hereford's Knob. No, I didn't make that up, honest. It's a great hill. It forms a part of the great northwest scarp of the Black Mountains and is a couple of miles west of the English border. This 2,260 feet high mountain is made of alternate layers of sandstone and mudstone dating from the Devonian period, which is about 400 million years old.

Gospel Pass & Hay Bluff

Above me is Hay Bluff, a flat summit, bordering England and Wales that overlooks the Wye Valley, and the book town of Hay-on-Wye below. The highest point of Hay Bluff is about 40 feet less than Twmpa.

I'm cycling along the Gospel Pass, which at 1,801 feet, is the highest road pass in Wales. The pass is supposed to have got its name from Saint Paul, the Roman

Jew who wrote over seven books for God's guidebook. He was brought through the pass by Caradog's daughter when he was doing a bit of preaching here.

The pass levels out at the top for a short distance, then carries on for a few miles. It's very popular with tourists but if you do decide to drive up here make sure you know how to reverse back down a 25% gradient and then do hill-starts to get going again as it's mostly single track along much of the eleven miles. Having said that there are numerous passing places too.

Lord Hereford's Knob

The area was also used in the opening scenes of the 1981 cult film 'An American Werewolf in London', a black comedy written by John Landis. It's a great film and yet another one where Jenny Agutter gets her kit off so not to be missed.

It's blowing a gale now and I'm aware that as well as sweating from the climb I'm now freezing cold. I pull my waterproof jacket on to warm up.

I take some more photos and wish I could stay longer but don't want it to get dark in case it's a full moon and the werewolves attack. I pedal on through the valley and I'm impressed at how big Lord Hereford's Knob is as I get closer to it. That joke was for Mark's benefit.

I pause for a final moment to watch the wind blow the clouds across the valley, then look above to see a sight, once common, that is becoming even more rare each year. A young female kestrel is riding the breeze like a child's kite. My spirits lift again and I can't resist tapping out a quick haiku on my iPhone.

Watching cloud shadow paint the ridge
sun playing hide and seek
kestrel hovers

Heading down

I keep left as the road forks and head for Capel y Ffin, which means chapel of the boundary. Built in 1762 the little Welsh chapel is one of the smallest in Wales. The village itself is famous because of its association with artist Eric Gill, who lived here with his followers between 1924-28. He designed the typefaces Gill Sans and Perpetua but should really be remembered for his diaries, where he kept explicit details of his sexual activities. He had sex with his daughters and a dog. I'll leave you to form your own opinions of the man.

I cycle on, downhill now, and what a downhill. Actually, it's a bit too steep and fast to enjoy as the road bends its way towards the valley bottom on its way to Llanthony Priory.

The country lanes are quite narrow and there are lots of potholes to negotiate but eventually the road flattens out a bit and you reach the Augustinian priory ruins.

Llanthony Priory dates back to 1100, when Walter de Lacy, a Norman nobleman came to the site and decided to chill out, shave a comedy circle off the top of his head and do a bit of monk stuff. By 1118 there were about forty of the black-cloaked lads living here. Further building work was done in 1325 and two years later Edward II stayed here on his way to Berkeley Castle to be murdered. He must have enjoyed his stay.

The ruins are Grade I listed buildings and run by Cadw. Entrance is free and there is a nice café here too. I stopped to take a photo but as I was only seven miles away from Abergavenny I didn't dwell for long. I didn't want any Edward II vibes to rub off on me that's for sure.

Llanthony Priory

I cycle on until I come to the village of Llanfihangel Crucorney. Famous for the Skirrid Mountain Inn, which claims to be one of the oldest pubs in Wales. Although some say the building is a 17th Century construction there was probably an inn of sorts on the site much earlier due to its proximity to the priory. I mean, we all know how those monks liked to knock it back so I'm happy to think the pub is over 900 years ago.

I grab a pint of Butty Bach and walk out the back to the beer garden where Owain Glyndŵr is said to have rallied his forces in the early 15th Century before raiding nearby settlements that supported King Henry IV.

Skirrid Inn

The first floor of the inn was also used as a Courtroom where capital punishment was carried out for certain offences, including sheep stealing. Local legend says that as many as 180 convicted criminals were hanged from an oak beam over the well of the staircase. Markings, possibly from rope marks, still exist on the staircase and if you're passing you can take a photo of yourself in a handy noose that's suddenly appeared at the bottom of the stairs before you enjoy the great real ale or local food.

Various ghost spotters (they're like bus spotters but wear Ghostbuster costumes not anoraks) claim the pub is home to several ghosts or spirits. There have also been numerous supernatural occurrences or paranormal activities recorded at the site, although Bill Murray hasn't verified them all yet.

Another popular myth surrounding the inn is that of the infamous Judge Jeffreys, the hanging judge, who is supposed to have heard cases here at the Courtroom. This is possible although he was probably only a wee lad of fourteen back then.

I drink my beer and chat to an English couple about the pub and the legends surrounding it for a bit. They are from Kidderminster and visiting family. The subject turns to immigrants and the Brexit vote as it always does these days. They tell me about the Muslims taking over areas of Birmingham, setting up Sharia courts and making parts of the city no-go areas for us infidels. I can't help thinking that the beam in the pub may be getting more use in years to come if the government keeps allowing this sort of thing to happen. I play devil's advocate for a bit but realise that there are real issues in many parts of the UK that have not really touched Wales yet.

I finish my pint, refreshed and happy to be just a few miles away from my digs. It's a nice B&B that Sue, my wife and tour operator, has found for me just on the outskirts of Abergavenny.

I say my goodbyes and jump back on the bike. I'm whizzing down the by-pass, doing 25mph when I see a turnoff. I head right and into Mardy. As I'm cycling downhill using Google Maps with one hand Warren rings. We have a quick chat but I have to find this guest house soon as it's getting late now.

I pull the brakes and come to a halt right outside the door of a B&B just as the little blue dots converge on my iPhone. Wow, I love technology sometimes, this is just so cool. I knock the door.

'Hi, I've got a room booked for tonight,' I confidently announce.

'What's the name please?' asks the puzzled looking man, who explains he's just covering for the owner and doesn't know much.

I wait for about ten minutes and he returns.

'What was your name again?'

I tell him and off he scurries.

'I'm sorry, there's no record of you? When did you book a room?'

'Oh, my wife rang up yesterday I think.'

'What's your name again?'

I felt like saying, 'It's not that bloody hard to remember!' but I refrained, smiled and repeated.

Twenty minutes had past now with me shivering in my sweaty clothes on the doorstep.

'What did you say your name was again?'

I was just about to lose it when I thought I'd show him my mobile and the text from Sue to say I had a room booked. This I did.

'Ah, that's not us. It's straight across the road, dead opposite, look,' he pointed to a small sign that said Park Guest House not The Black Lion, which I was stood outside.

I had to laugh. I was just about to rip him a new one but instead apologised profusely and pushed my bike across Hereford Road with my tail between my legs.

The food of athletes!

I had a quick shower, put my wonderfully accurate gadgets on charge and went out. I walked into town and topped up the carbohydrates again. Sue rang to say the

193

local newspaper would be turning up to welcome me home on Thursday.

Abergavenny is a friendly, market town a few miles from the English border. The town dates back to the Iron Age when it was an important iron-smelting place. The Brythonic word for blacksmith is Gobannia (river of blacksmiths) and is where the town and river gets its name. The town is surrounded by two mountains, the Blorenge and Sugar Loaf, both fairly easy walks you can do in a single day.

Beer time

I visited the Hen and Chicks for a nice pint of Rev James Gold and listened to two old men trying to chat up a young girl who seemed to have an obsession with living in Spain and kept showing them photos on her phone of all the places she'd been. All one of them. Bit weird.

I left them to it and wandered down to the Wetherspoons where I was very tempted to have a second meal but instead settled for a disgusting pint of Exmoor Gold, which was practically undrinkable. I decided Tuesday night wasn't going to be that lively so headed home, surprised at how cold it had become outside, especially in August. I paid a visit to a local shop and got a hot, microwaved pastie to warm me up.

I was walking home to the B&B when I passed The Bailey. I looked inside and decided it wouldn't hurt to have one more. It didn't hurt too much, although Worthy Best isn't my favourite beer.

I sat on my own in the corner until a local lad started talking to me about my cycling trip. Shane Lewis of Lewis Taxis gave me £20 to give to Prostate Cancer UK. I thanked him and we started chatting about all the wildlife I'd seen on my trip so far. Shane was very knowledgeable about nature and was also a member of the Royal Pigeon Racing Association, of which he was proud to tell me The Queen was patron.

Our inbred Royal family first got into racing pigeons in 1886 when King Leopold II of Belgium gave some to the family to start a racing loft on the Sandringham Estate. Both King Edward VII and King George V enjoyed racing their pigeons and many of these prized birds were used as carrier pigeons during both world wars.

Racing pigeons are descended from the Rock Dove, and were even used by Ramses III to convey news between cities regarding the flood state of the River Nile. The Romans also used pigeons as messengers for war and the Olympics.

Whilst I had to admit to a certain ignorance regarding the sport, I do know a little bit about zoology, having studied at Cardiff University. Me and Shane chatted for ages about the merits of preserving one type of raptor over another, he spoke passionately, intelligently and sympathetically about wildlife conservation. He'd seen a goshawk take a kestrel, got heartbroken when his pet robin got killed by a sparrowhawk and wasn't a huge fan of peregrines. He also tried to dispel the myth that pigeon racers are all poisoners and campaigned for a more level playing field for all wild birds of prey.

I walked home, knackered and slept like a baby dreaming of Marina and the Diamonds, who was born in the town, dressed up in a sexy bird costume. I suppose I could point out that dreaming of birds symbolises hope, aspiration, joy, harmony and love. Then again maybe I was just thinking about something else. I mean, have you seen her?

Cycling Stats

Start: 9:00am
Distance: 66.82 miles
Total Distance: 610.28 miles
Average Speed: 10.62mph
Fastest Speed: 35.46mph
Cycling Time: 6 hrs 17 mins
Finish: 7:00pm
Calories: 4794
Ascent: 5144 ft
Descent: 5518 ft
Beers: 4

Route

Hill Profile

 # Day 13

Abergavenny to Chepstow
Wednesday 10th August 2016

iPhone alarm: Freebird – Lynard Skynard

After a nice breakie at the B&B (the right one) I bimble around town looking for photos to represent the town but nothing really grabs me. I take some cash out of the hole in the wall (with more success than Mark) and who should be stood next to me but the ramblers group leader from Knighton. It's a small world all right.

I check my mobile because a college mate, Adrian, got in touch a week back after thirty years of him travelling the world to say he was back in Wales and wouldn't mind doing a day or two with me. Nothing yet though.

On the bike I retrace my route back up Hereford Road and see that some bright spark has mowed the grass in the mountain to spell out 'Croeso', which is Welsh for welcome.

I text a few mates to see if they'll be around for a beer on Thursday, when I hopefully finish in one piece, and wait for the replies. Meanwhile I cycle up a hill following the blue signs again (Route 42) and am soon exploring the hills around this beautiful part of Gwent.

Croeso

I'm heading up the lanes, happy in the knowledge that today is my shortest day of the whole trip when I realise that I probably had too much beer last night. It's a funny thing, drinking. One or two beers the night before I find is fine. I get up, get some food down my neck and I'm away, but once you have three or four the next day is hard, especially the first few hours.

Thankfully it's not too bad a day, not too hot, not too cold and the climbs are fairly easy compared to yesterday's Tenzing Norgay hills over the Gospel Pass. I tell myself my tired legs are due to that rather than the beers. Yeh definitely that.

199

I listen to rabbits nibbling away in the fields as my tyres clack over hazelnut shells. There's a book title in there I think to myself – 'Cycling Over Hazelnut Shells' or something? Bugger, I promised Simon I'd use 'Wales Trails' now. And I have the t-shirt.

I push on east and at the top of a small hill I stop to take a photo of Sugar Loaf way off in the distance. I think back to almost exactly a year ago when me, Warren and John, pedalled our mountain bikes to the top of the mountain. It was a lovely day and a lovely ride. Then I made the mistake of riding down. Not from the top mind you, even we were sensible enough not to do that, but from just below the summit. We bombed through the dirt tracks and heather until 'bang!' A split-second later I'm looking like Peter Griffin after a fight with a chicken. I'm in a ditch with my *cboardman* carefully balanced, upside down on the ledge next to me. My neck was at a funny angle but I could still wiggle my toes.

Sugar Loaf

Luckily for me the Bell helmet saved my life (it was actually cracked right through) and Warren and John's First Aid certificates were thankfully up to date. I pedal on and think how near yet how far I am from home.

200

I'm admiring the lovely views of the valley below when my lower intestinal tract decides it's about time to rebel against the two-week diet of high sugar drinks, curry and meat. Definitely not the beer, that's all organic surely?

Having cycled uphill a fair way I'm rewarded with a few, fast downhills. One of these I take a bit too quickly and near the bottom, just as I'm accelerating out of a bend I nearly get Jacob'd (cream crackers) by a poor farmer in his £80,000 Range Rover. I suddenly think back to the accident a year ago.

I push on and also push back. I'm getting really desperate for a pit stop now. I have plenty of serviettes from the chippy in my pannier, plus some wet-wipes and an abundance of quiet, secluded fields... dare I?

I take a photo of a great sign on a farmhouse wall and wonder if I should just take a dump here? It would be a talking point if nothing else.

Nothing yet!

I hope Raglan has a toilet as well as a castle and cycle on.

Another series of up and down and I nearly come off going over some rough potholes before almost getting creamed again, this time by a brand new Freelander.

'Oh dear, that's twice now,' I say to myself. 'Just need an Evogue to complete the three.'

I get to a main road and have a choice to make. I can keep going to Raglan or turn right to follow Route 42 to Usk. As I'm wondering which way is best a local farmer stops and has a chat. He tells me the way I'm thinking of going is steep and I'll end up pushing. I smile and assure him I'll be OK, especially after yesterday. He nods and drives off laughing to himself.

I carry on and follow the river for a while on a nice flat section and soon reach the small, old Roman town of Usk. I cycle through town and find they have an 'Arkwrights' shop just like the one in Taffs Well, where David Jason used to visit his girlfriend many years ago.

High Street

The River Usk has a stone bridge, built in 1750 by William Edwards, who also built the Old Bridge in Pontypridd. The town can probably be mentioned for many other things and I'm sure Owain Glyndŵr burnt it to the ground like everywhere else he ever visited but for me at this particular moment in time it only had one purpose – the public toilet.

I lock the bike up just in case there's any light-fingered millionaires about and venture inside, pleased that

202

there is no charge to use the facilities. There was no toilet paper (not a problem, I always carry my own), plenty of soap but no water or air from the hand dryer but I shall always be eternally grateful.

One thing I must say though, whilst going through the motions, I couldn't help notice that there was a fair amount of felt pen scribbling on the wall. It was most illuminating to read about Tim and his more than adequate number of inches. It took me back to a bygone age, although to be honest I thought the Internet and rainbow flags outside old pubs had consigned all that kind of stuff to history? Ah well, onwards I went with the sun shining all around me.

Usk Bridge

I'm enjoying the cycling now and notice that for the fourth day running I'm accompanied by buzzard calls 'keow, keow' and I cast my mind back to last night and the chat with Shane and also my alarm call this morning with Ronnie Van Zant and Allen Collins awesome lyrics:

If I leave here tomorrow
Would you still remember me
For I must be travelin' on now
There's too many places I got to see

I'm travelling on all right and if all goes to plan my 600+ mile ride around Wales will be over tomorrow. I feel quite sad to think I'll soon be home, chained to a desk and my crappy iMac, buggered since I installed El Crapitan on it. But at least I'm free now I think to myself as I cycle past Usk prison.

I push through some more nice lanes, then a big, long hill that's easily rideable, although it's quite steep at the top. Mark rings to update me on the latest news from home and to give me a roundup of the Olympic rugby sevens matches.

Although I'm someone who normally likes to watch the news I've really enjoyed not hearing the usual bad news on TV these last two weeks. I've also not missed constantly checking emails and listening to Mister Gupter from Bangalore trying to sell me everything from BT broadband to his sister.

Stunning scenery

I'm half way up a nice big hill when a jeep slows down and stops next to me. I think my lucks in but instead a very horsey, country casual type of woman tells me that I'm really hard to see and that I need some Hi-Vis on.

I'm so shocked that she's driven off before I have time to say 'Oh thanks love, maybe tomorrow I'll wear my

DayGlo Spiderman costume and stick a pink feather up my...'

I guess I should appreciate the advice and not be so annoyed but part of me wants to scream 'Well get your bloody eyes tested love!' seeing as I'm 6ft 3ins, 16st and it's the middle of a sunny day.

I get to the top of this hill and discover some nice woodland walks that Tim from Usk would have liked. Then it's back on the Dawes for a very fast and dangerous downhill past an empty reservoir and the first sight of the Bristol Channel about nine or ten miles out of Chepstow.

I whizz on, speeding down another hill and almost have a head-on with an old, red, Series II Landie – OK, let that be my third and final, hairy moment today please. Perhaps 'Margot' in her jeep had a point?

I soon reach the main road and checking both ways for any Romans stop to water the hedge at Caerwent. It's then that I notice someone has thrown away one of those giant, blue Ikea bags. I'm getting the feeling this is the really posh, and rich, part of Wales. I mean, those things are like gold dust in the valleys! No way would anyone throw one of them away. In fact I remember a time when Mark even wore one to the top of Pen-Y-Fan.

I'm on the last bit of today's ride now, on a cycle lane, alongside the main road when I see the Celtic Trail, Route 4 sign. I follow that through some nice, rolling lanes with a few little, twisty turny bits thrown in just to annoy you when you are so agonisingly close and then it goes all Pete Tong.

I'm following a maze of signs, directions, route number swaps and loops through A roads, housing estates and country lanes. It's ridiculous, which way am I supposed to be going? Is this just here to confuse me I wonder? I guess all the routes must end at Chepstow? Either that or the zombie apocalypse has started and it's Sustrans way of telling us to stay in Wales. Don't go any further! Don't cross the border!

I give up on the last mile and just follow my nose into town. I cycle around the back of the castle and drop down the hill into the bottom of Chepstow town by the river.

I meet Sue in the Three Tuns beer garden and have a pint of pale ale.

'Good day?' asks Sue.

'Yeh, easy really, even my knees work.'

One more day to go

We have a quick catch up and head back to the pub for a shower and to lock the bike away out back. The George was built around 1620 and is positioned just outside the town walls. The Gate House was positioned on the other side and some people think tunnels may have linked the two buildings.

It's not a bad place to stay, very central and we've been here before a couple of times. This time I managed to get a special offer Groupon deal, a double room, bed and breakfast for £39, with a free bottle of Prosecco thrown in. I booked it online, then added a £10 off voucher I found and we got the room for £29, sorted!

I did the unpacking ceremony for the last time and we went downstairs to the bar. I plumped for the fish, chips, giant onion rings and peas and Sue had some girly thing I couldn't pronounce. The Prosecco was absent though so we had a free bottle of white wine instead. Suitably replenished we hit the town.

Chepstow is a lovely, Welsh town, just a stone's throw away from England across the River Wye, which has one of the highest tidal ranges in the world. It's the nearest, large town to the southern most point of Offa's Dyke, which begins on the east bank of the river at Sedbury Cliffs in England. It is thought the dyke was built in the 8th Century to keep the mad Welsh out of Mercia but now a cast iron bridge links Gwent with Gloucestershire. I'm not sure King Offa would have approved.

Old Wye Bridge

We walked around town and made our way down to the river. I took a photo of a picturesque tile display showing another loop of Wales – the Offa's Dyke walk, which is 177 miles long and the Welsh Coastal Walk, which is 870 miles long. I'm walking the Offa's Dyke path with my daughter and cycled past the end point at Prestatyn a few days back. If you join the two paths together you've got well over 1,000 miles of walking around the whole of the country! Maybe next year?

Humans have actually been around this part of Wales for 7,000 years of course and even though the Romans established Caerwent as a trading centre 5,000 years later many believe Chepstow might have been used by both Saxons and the Welsh prior to this.

I take a photo of the castle, which is the oldest surviving, post-Roman, stone fortification in all of Britain with the oldest castle doors in Europe. Built on the cliffs above the river its construction began in 1067, just a year after William the Conqueror invaded the UK, such was the importance of the site to Norman occupation. Chepstow Castle is also the most southerly of a chain of castles built in the Welsh Marches.

Wales Loop

We visit my favourite pub in Chepstow, the Five Alls for another real ale, we listen to Guns N' Roses, Metallica and Rainbow on the jukebox and play a couple of games of pool. How else does a true athlete wind down the night before the last day of an epic cycling adventure?

The town is also famous (or should that be infamous?) for The Widders Border Morris Men who are mostly bikers looking like the 'Black Widows' from Clint Eastwood's film *Every Which Way but Loose*. They are a sort of rock n roll, punky, Morris dancing troupe. We walk home and try to avoid bumping into anyone from the dark side of Morris dancing and wish Oliver Cromwell was still in charge because he banned all this sort of thing.

I try to have an early night in readiness for the final push tomorrow but Sue insisted on watching the Olympics,

208

and Mock the Week, while drinking full fat, milk and crunching loudly on a jumbo size packet of bacon crisps. And they say romance is dead.

Chepstow Castle

Cycling Stats

Start: 9:00am
Distance: 30.84 miles
Total Distance: 641.12 miles
Average Speed: 9.84mph
Fastest Speed: 28.53mph
Cycling Time: 3 hrs 09 mins
Finish: 2:50pm
Calories: 2287
Ascent: 3153 ft
Descent: 3199 ft
Beers: 2
Wine: 2½

Route

Hill Profile

 # Day 14

Chepstow to Pontypridd
Thursday 11th August 2016

iPhone alarm: Life is a Long Song – Jethro Tull

Woke up with the usual bad back then after the ritual stretching, moaning and packing (minus a few clothes that Sue will take in the car) we pop downstairs for a huge, final breakie, which makes me feel a bit like the condemned man. I hope not, those Landies were too close for comfort yesterday.

Final push

We grab a final photo opportunity at the back of the pub and then I'm off. After the last couple of miles of confusion yesterday I decide to skip the first part of Route 4 today. Instead I just annoy the rush hour lorries on the steep hill out of town. It's a bit dodgy on a few bends but after half an hour on the busy A48 I reach the top of the hill and at a roundabout turn left towards Caldicot. I stop for a photo of the Severn Bridge in the distance. Then a few miles later I follow the signs for Caldicot castle.

During Henry I of England's reign the castle was probably just a simple motte-and-bailey but it was rebuilt in stone around 1100. It eventually fell into ruins before being repaired as late as 1885. This probably explains why it looks so good now.

It's an impressive Norman fortification and can be easily found by cycling past the Asda superstore, the Curry Mahal, then turn right past the New Garden Chinese takeaway and massage parlour and you're there. Nice pub too.

Caldicot Castle

I stop for a few photos and an energy bar washed down with the last of my Lucozade store. I make it back to the main road as the wind starts to pick up and continue until I take a left at the train station.

This brings you back onto the Celtic Trail that runs all the way to the city of Newport. The road goes under the railway at this point so be careful because the clearance is not good. The first time I cycled under this bridge I thought we must be going the wrong way. It's only about five foot high so you have to duck big time, especially if you're six foot three like me!

You then cross a road bridge but it's worth a quick pause because the trail takes you over the M4 motorway. The Severn Bridge tolls are on the Welsh side of the border and some say it's not really fair that we Welsh must pay to get back into our own country. Others don't really care.

Severn Toll

Having saved two or three pints worth of beer money by avoiding the tolls you find yourself on a very flat and featureless section. There is a horrible, straight gravel track next which is more suitable to mountain bikes but my trusty Dawes, the pride of British engineering, takes it in its stride.

Although not obvious while cycling, this area of the south coast of Wales is dominated by reens, or drainage ditches. This fen-like landscape is of human construction, probably begun by the Romans and continued into medieval times.

The coastal lands were reclaimed from the Severn Estuary and Bristol Channel and are part of the Caldicot and Wentloog Levels. The reens were built to help prevent flooding and drain any excess water off the low-lying fields and carry it to the sea.

Worth a stop on this part of the route is St Thomas the Apostle's church, at Redwick, a Grade I listed building. The old porch has a mark that shows the height of the famous Bristol Channel flood of 1607. The village was about 2m underwater! Oh, how us Pontypridd rugby fans would like to see those days return.

The church is also famous for having two of its six bells dating from 1350, which makes them the oldest working church bells anywhere in the country.

St Thomas Church

Redwick is also worth a stop for The Rose Inn pub, which does chips if you catch the owner on a good day. There's an interesting old millstone in a shed next to the church too.

The wind is picking up now, just as the weather forecast said it would. OK *Benny*, let's just call it one-all in the ice cream league shall we? I cycle on into a 15mph headwind along flat lanes as the road bends slowly up towards the River Usk and the city of Newport.

If you have the time it's well worth a visit to the RSPB Nature Reserve, known locally as the 'wetlands' in Nash. It's not far from the cycle trail. There is a café, shop and plenty of walks. Bird hides can be used to look at and photograph all manner of warblers and wildfowl and there is a nice walk down to the estuary where the East Usk Lighthouse stands.

If you're a birder then you may want to look for lapwings, redshanks, plovers, teal, oystercatchers, shovellors, bitterns, hen harriers, owls and even the odd rare glossy ibis. They've all been seen here.

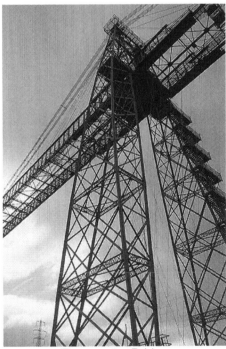
Transporter Bridge

The roads are flat and fast now, even with the wind against me and I turn into a little wooded area near two wind turbines. I exit onto a busier road, pass some factories and make my way to the world famous Newport Transporter Bridge.

215

The Transporter Bridge is one of only eight in the world still working and is a Grade I listed structure. It is also the oldest and largest of the three transporter bridges left in Britain. The distance between the centres of the anchorage caissons is 1,545 feet. The toll for a cyclist and his bike is £1. I did think the man in the Hi-Vis yellow and official-looking peak cap might have waived the fee seeing as I'm doing the ride for charity but alas I had to settle for a photo from him instead.

You could cycle around the bridge by heading north but the National Cycle Network and Celtic Trail actually uses the bridge and it's also where Route 47 begins.

Crossing the River Usk in style

After the obligatory photos are taken it's across the busy road on the pedestrian crossing and a swift pedal through the delightful little hamlet of Pill before you start to see a few blue signs again. You could break up your ride by stopping here and spending the night. Especially if you've just returned from hand-to-hand fighting against Al Qaeda in the Tora Bora caves. Gwent Police have proposed a plan to develop a designated area for prostitution within the boundaries of Pill and there are some great pubs if you want to reacquire what customs confiscated off you at Kabul airport.

You can also detour into the centre of Newport, the third largest city in Wales, where the trail splits into two and heads either to Cross Keys and Risca (a great ride past the canals) or to Caerphilly (over the hills and past numerous farms before dropping down to the famous castle). Both these routes are fantastic sections but they avoid the capital city of Wales, Cardiff.

The area around Newport has seen humans living there since the Bronze Age and the famous Roman fort at Caerleon marks the edge of their empire. This is a great day out especially if you have kids who like to play with swords.

Also worth a look is the 5th Century St Woolos Church, which became Newport Cathedral in 1949 and is also Grade I listed.

It was during the industrial revolution that Newport really came into its own though. The exploitation of the south Wales valleys meant merchants needed ports in which to transport their coal and iron across the world. By 1830 Newport was exporting more coal than Cardiff.

On 4 November 1839 Newport went down in history though. It was the place where the last large-scale armed rebellion against authority in Great Britain took place. Soldiers opened fire on 10,000 protestors outside the Westgate Hotel and killed twenty-two demonstrators. It was one of the largest civil massacres committed by the British government in the 19th Century.

The leaders of the rebellion, including John Frost, were convicted and sentenced to a traitor's death. The sentence was later commuted to transportation to Australia.

Many famous people have called the city their home over the years, including Johnny Morris of Animal Magic, actor Michael Sheen, and the supertramp poet W. H. Davies, who wrote:

'What is this life if, full of care,
We have no time to stand and stare'

I didn't have time to stand or stare either as I was determined to blaze a trail to Cardiff, west from Newport, seeing as the Sustrans lot hadn't managed it yet.

I followed the trail past Halfords, along Docks Way and passed under the main road to Lighthouse Road where I headed south for St Brides rather than continue to Tredegar House. This was a gamble and I was now in uncharted territory having cycled both the other trails on previous rides.

I pedalled on to Peterstone where the flat floodplains below the M4 and A48 are a different world. I was now in an area of Wales few people ever see because of our obsession with speed, convenience and time. Given the chance of driving from *A to B* how many of us choose a motorway rather than an A road? As for old B roads that take us to the same place, how many of us are prepared to sacrifice a few minutes of our lives in order to be less stressed out and experience more of our natural environment? Everyone is in such a rush these days and it can't be good for us.

I was enjoying the solitude but like all good things it quickly came to an end as I entered one of the worst parts of Wales I'd ever experienced. Gone the peace and quiet, suddenly I see a signpost that made me ashamed to be Welsh. It said 'Welcome to Wales' but was broken, vandalised, spray-painted and filthy dirty. I cruise slowly on. At first it's like *28 Days Later*, then I feel like I'm in a remake of *Escape from New York* with Kurt Russell doing his best Clint Eastwood impression.

I come upon a caravan site. There are loads of vans, you can't miss them, there's rubbish everywhere, dogs barking and burnt out cars.

Maybe this is why Sustrans haven't put any blue signs up down here? They'd be stolen for scrap in an hour. I cycle on, steering around discarded nappies, coke cans and other detritus left on the road. I see a young mother, still in pyjamas. It's 1:00pm in the afternoon and I feel like I've been transported to the *Jungle* migrant camp in Calais. Roll on Splott.

Then it gets crazy. I enter an industrial area and try to keep left, watching out for impatient lorry drivers and ignore the signs for Newport that are pointing to Cardiff. I just carry on. I'm almost in the capital, I can feel it in the air. I'm so near yet so far. The traffic is suddenly horrendous. It seems to come from nowhere. I try to cycle with it for a mile or so but the cement dust burns my eyes. I take ten minutes to cross the road to get to a pavement. No one will slow down for me to rush across the road. Bastards! What is wrong with these people?

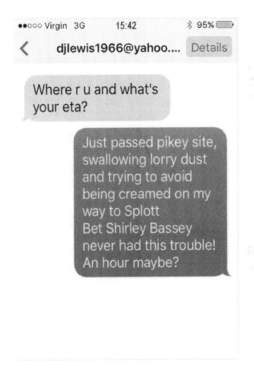

Eventually I manage to thread my way through a few short cycle lanes, over some bridges and I'm on to the shopping nightmare of Newport Road. I turn left past the fantastic Royal Oak pub and reach the relative safety of Mogadishu (sorry that should read Splott).

Cardiff has always had a large Muslim population and the first mosque in the UK was opened in Cathays in 1860. Over half of all Welsh Muslims live in the city.

I decided to revisit Adamsdown, as I used to live there thirty years ago whilst at University, and cycled along the street known as Broadway. The change in an area was quite startling. Dirty, run-down streets where once it was a thriving, friendly, multicultural place. Most of the great old pubs are now shut, businesses are closed and there's rubbish piled up everywhere.

I abandon my dreams of reliving the past and cycle the short distance to the city centre for some lunch, although you could just as easy go to the Bay from here.

Cardiff is the capital of Wales and also the largest city. Even so only 350,000 people live in the unitary authority. A popular tourist destination, the centre is a vibrant, friendly city especially during big sporting events, like the Six Nations, when the city centre pubs are full to bursting point.

Human beings have lived here for at least 6,000 years. To put this into context that is 1,500 years before Stonehenge or the Great Pyramid of Giza. Iron Age forts and settlements can be found in many areas and Cardiff is known to have been part of the Silures territory that stretched to Brecon and Monmouth.

The Romans came of course, around 75 AD but left a few hundred years later. No one really knows what happened then but I imagine the Welsh just got back to drinking beer, womanising and fighting. Then the Normans arrived.

Cardiff Castle was built on the site of the old Roman fort around 1081 although it was greatly altered into what can be seen today in Victorian times. English settlers moved in and the town grew. Probably as a result of this our hero, Owain Glyndŵr, burned Cardiff and took possession of the Castle in 1404. As many buildings were made of timber, much of Cardiff was destroyed. A statue of him was erected in Cardiff Town Hall in the early 20th Century. And why not I say!

I decided I needed a drink after my brief encounter with the past so stopped outside one of the best rugby pubs in the world. What better way to toast Owain? I chat to a divorced IT guy, who used to work in London before his wife stole his life's savings and buggered off. We have ten minutes on the meaning of life and I look back on the last two weeks with some satisfaction.

Old Arcade

Although I'll be heading north on the Taff Trail it's worth mentioning the Battle of St Fagans that took place during the English Civil War. The Welsh Royalists lost to the New Model Army and so Cromwell basically conquered Wales as a result. Some might ask why the poor Welsh worker would support the Crown but in those days religion was a major influencer on whose side you picked. If you were an Anglican or Catholic you'd tend to support the Royalists but also many landowners forced their workers to side with them. As a result many poor Welshmen had no choice but to side with the posh gits who'd screw them over the first chance they got. You'd think people would learn. from history wouldn't you?

Cardiff Castle

The modern city of Cardiff was built by John Crichton-Stuart, the 2nd Marquis of Bute. Well, not actually by him, more likely his poor Welsh slaves. He created Cardiff Docks, which linked to the Taff Vale Railway, and by the 1830s Cardiff became the major port for exporting coal from the south Wales valleys.

The 'valleys' we know today grew by 80% over a thirty year period, much of it due to migration from within Wales. Cardiff however still had a quarter of its population English born. The city grew and overtook Swansea and Merthyr in size and in 1893 my old University was built.

Devolution came, narrowly, in 1997 and we've got poorer ever since. Lagging behind all the other home nations in wealth, job opportunities and most importantly hope. Having said this Wales has never voted for a Conservative government so maybe independence is the answer if we truly want to control our own destiny?

Plenty of famous people have come from Cardiff of course and you do wonder why some of the more affluent don't seem to want to become involved in politics in order to improve the lot of their fellow Welsh men and women.

Authors Ken Follett and Roald Dahl were born here of course as was pirate Henry Morgan, journalist Jeremy Bowen, creator of the Daleks Terry Nation, footballers Gareth Bale and Ryan Giggs, boxers Jim Driscoll and Steve Robinson and show jumper David Broome.

They say Wales is the land of song and so it's not surprising that singers Charlotte Church, Shirley Bassey, Ivor Novello and Cerys Matthews all come from the city.

Wales today is still a divided nation, albeit a tiny one. Cardiff is quite prosperous while the south Wales valleys just a few miles north are some of the poorest areas in the UK.

I finish my beer and look forward to seeing this area soon, as it's where I started my ride just under two weeks ago. I'm almost home and fancy another pint in Pontypridd now. I say goodbye to my new friend and get ready for the final few miles.

I take a quick photo of the castle, nice and grey today as the wind starts to pick up again and I'm off. I cycle up the pavement towards the Welsh College of Music and soon turn left away from the main road and back onto the Taff Trail.

This is an area I know well and I make good time as I head through Bute Park, past Llandaf Rowing Club, before stopping for a drink of water at the salmon weir. I get off my bike and lean it on the bench then look at the raging waters of the Taff and wonder, as I always do, how on earth a fish can jump and swim up that!

I'm enjoying the sound of the river when a high-pitched giggling noise makes me turn around. Behind me are three, very attractive, scantily clad young girls in bikinis or something (not burkinis that's for sure) and a female photographer snapping away. I think about going over and telling them I'm a photographer too but then I think better of it seeing as there is no-one else about and I don't want to hear them screaming 'Help, paedo!' if I try a spot of banter with them. I get back on my bike and pedal off.

I get to Tonygwynlais and consider stopping for a beer at the Lewis Arms but instead take a quick snap of the pub with the 'fairy castle' in the background. It might just be me but whenever I see Castell Coch, especially from the A470 after a trip away somewhere, I always feel I'm 'home'. It's a symbol, a marker, a point of reference that signifies the end of the city and the start of the green hills and valleys that we call home. I send Sue a text to say I'm almost there, but just have to check my hair for the newspapers before I cycle on.

Castell Coch in the background

I'm heading north on Route 8, the fifty-five mile walking and cycling trail that runs from Cardiff to Brecon. It's a trail I know well having cycled it many times over the years but this time it seems so dull as all I want to do is finish and have a pint.

The Taff Trail is anything but dull of course and passes through some stunning scenery, with fascinating history and is mostly off road too. A cyclist's dream, especially compared to some of the more haphazard experiments I've made during the last fortnight.

I pause for a quick photo of the signpost I never normally stop at and see I have only a few miles left of my adventure. No, a tear isn't forming, honest.

224

The last few miles are easy, there's a nice, long, gentle hill just before the detour to Caerphilly and the castle but I'm not feeling particularly medieval at the moment, although I can smell hops and malt.

Taff Trail

I phone Sue again to make sure the local rag is there, after all this must be a huge story for them, thinking about the rubbish they normally print these days.

'Hi, are the boys there? I did text them all,' I ask.

'No, no one yet,' replied my wife.

'Ah, what about the paper?'

'No, they haven't turned up either, about right for them though.'

'Great, didn't want a fuss anyway.'

I cycle on, through Ynysangharad War Memorial Park and cross the road to the Llanover Arms. Suddenly a huge shout goes up as Sue, Eve, her friend Caragh, my mam, Aunty Al, Babs and Janine all jump into the street waving flags and Prostate Cancer UK banners.

'Are you tired Dave?' someone asks.

'No, just fancy a pint really,' I reply as enthusiastic as ever.

I get bombarded with twenty questions from all the women who then proceed to answer all the twenty

225

questions before I have chance to think of a suitable answer for the first one...

We take a few photos and settle down to some real ale. I've made it home to Pontypridd, the old, run-down market town famous for its Old Bridge across the River Taff and its fantastic rugby team that I know and love.

Finish Line

Pontypridd town was a rural backwater before coal was discovered in the valleys in the mid 18th Century. It then grew rapidly like many of the surrounding towns and villages but after Thatcher closed everything down it has since drifted aimlessly into poverty and social deprivation. It has just about recaptured the 'backwater' accolade helped along by the backward council and the last couple of MPs, the latest of which, Owen Smith, has just stood for Labour leader! Once a thriving town surrounded by several collieries now the only real employers are local government, the justice system and the health service.

The town has had an illustrious past though with many world famous people hailing from the immediate area. Opera singers Stuart Burrows and Geraint Evans came from my own village, Cilfynydd, just a mile north of here whilst old, layabout Tom Jones came from a mile south.

226

William Price is probably the most interesting character to be associated with Pontypridd and I often think we need more like him. He was a druid, doctor, Welsh nationalist, vegetarian, naturist, Chartist and made cremation legal in the UK when he burnt the body of his five-month old son, Jesus Christ, on Llantrisant Common.

The list of Welsh rugby internationals to come from Pontypridd is long and getting longer, although most people will already know about Neil Jenkins, Russell Robbins and Tommy David.

Although proud of where I come from it has to be said that the valleys are declining as people leave to look for work and better lives elsewhere. Over 90% of residents were born here making it one of the least diverse places in Wales, if not the UK.

Llanover Arms

The valleys have a high teenage pregnancy rate and school achievement is low. Many people have long-term health problems even though the Taff Trail offers a fabulous opportunity to get fit and enjoy the fresh air. The area also has a high unemployment rate.

Having said this though the town's watering holes are very hospitable and welcoming. You'll certainly have a laugh if you drop in to the Wonky, Clwb Y Bont or the *Llan* on the weekend and start chatting to the friendly locals. Unless you bump into me of course and I'll just ask you to buy a novel or something.

And so on that happy note... I'm thrilled to be back and settle down to my long-awaited beer, get lots of 'girly' comments about how much weight I've lost and how good I'm looking, which just makes me think that everyone must have considered me a fat, ugly bastard before I set out. I drown my sorrows in four more wonderful pints.

I have one last photo, cycle up the hill to the house and order a curry from the local takeaway. I have a shower, unpack my panniers and notice I have one Lidl chewy bar left.

'What great planning!' I say to myself. 'Derek would be proud!'

I sit down, relax, crack open a bottle of real ale and then Mark rings.

'What's happening? Are you back yet?'

Cycling Stats

Start: 9:00am
Distance: 47.17 miles
Total Distance: 688.29 miles
Average Speed: 9.43mph
Fastest Speed: 30.82mph
Cycling Time: 5 hrs 00 mins
Finish: 5:00pm
Calories: 2628
Ascent: 2323 ft
Descent: 2208 ft
Beers: 6
Curry: 1

Route

Hill Profile

Statistics

Day	Distance (Miles)	Ascent (Feet)
1	59.02	3900
2	66.41	4856
3	44.03	4157
4	-	-
5	70.09	5554
6	55.83	3399
7	42.04	2611
8	64.23	3681
9	43.77	2218
10	54.21	3599
11	43.83	3284
12	66.82	5144
13	30.84	3153
14	47.17	2323
Total	**688.29**	**47878**

While the distance might not be that impressive (almost as far as Cardiff to Munich) the ascent is quite interesting:

I cycled / climbed 1.65 times the height of Mount Everest (or 13.45 times the height of Y Wyddfa).

Final Thoughts

Although I had to lose a day from my planned route due to bike problems I still managed to cycle 688 miles around Wales and raised over £500 (to date) for Prostate Cancer UK.

Regrets? I've had a few... if I'd had more time (or been fitter) I would have cycled right down and around the gorgeous Llŷn peninsula, maybe done a lap of Ynys Môn to discover yet more lanes plus a few beaches and also east to Monmouth for a beer there as well. Other than that I was pretty satisfied with the 'loop' of Wales I managed.

This book has many uses of course. It can be used as a 'very' rough guide for those wishing to repeat, or more likely improve upon, my journey. It can be given to someone who seldom leaves their armchair as inspiration to get out and do something, 'cos if I can do it I'm sure anyone can! But lastly, and I hope, most importantly, this book is for those that realise that Wales may just be the final frontier. Just think Cuba, Tibet and Star Trek. We really are so small that we might not be here forever. So get on your bike and pay us a visit before we get overrun and have our unique, beautiful, wacky culture swallowed up by our pesky neighbours.

Land's End to John o' Groats is an iconic cycle ride that many bikers have done but who has done a circuit of Wales? Maybe this book can go someway to turn Wales into a sort of LEJOG-lite? It's a lot shorter, 650 miles up against 900 miles, so why not? You only need one lift not two, because it's a circle. You can start and finish wherever you fancy? If you have two weeks holiday then why not give it a go? You might like it.

Oh yeh, and tell your friends or give them this book. No actually, don't do that. Ask them to buy a copy ☺

References

The Celtic Trail by Rob Penn, paperback, 88 pages, Pocket Mountains Ltd. & Sustrans (2008)

Lôn Cambria & Lôn Teifi by Rob Penn, bilingual paperback, 112 pages, Pocket Mountains Ltd. & Sustrans (2011)

A few printed maps of North Wales, from an old Aldi Road Atlas, which I threw away when I'd cycled off that page.

iPhone, Google Maps for the many, many times I got lost.

DuckDuckGo instead of *Evil Google*, so I could check my facts regards the towns and history stuff when writing this account up.

Charities

Prostate Cancer UK
www.prostatecanceruk.org

Prostate Cancer Wales & UK
www.prostatecancerwales.co.uk

Just Giving
www.justgiving.com/fundraising/WalesTrails

Dave Lewis is from Cilfynydd, South Wales. He has always lived in Wales except for a year in Kenya.

He has published thirteen books to date, and this is his second cycling book.

He is founder and organiser of The Welsh Poetry Competition, an international competition that seeks to encourage and nurture talented writers that have been overlooked by the arts establishment in Wales.

Please pass the link on to anyone who fancies jumping on a bike to do the same ride, because the aim of the ride (and this book) is to put Wales on the cycling map as an alternative (or addition) to the other great iconic cycle rides in the UK, in particular LEJOG.

If you liked this paperback and could find five minutes to leave a positive review on Amazon, Dave would be thrilled.

And finally, good luck to anyone that does the ride – we hope you have as much fun as we did.

For more information about the author and to see his other work please visit his web site.

By the same author:

Poetry:
Layer Cake © 2009
Urban Birdsong © 2010
Sawing Fallen Logs For Ladybird Houses © 2011
Haiku © 2012
Roadkill © 2013
Reclaiming The Beat © 2016

Novels:
Ctrl-Alt-Delete © 2011
Raising Skinny Elephants © 2013
iCommand © 2015

Edited:
Welsh Poetry Competition Anthology © 2011

Non-Fiction:
Photography Composition © 2014
Land's End to John o' Groats © 2015
Wales Trails © 2016

Websites:
www.david-lewis.co.uk
www.davelewisphotography.co.uk
www.welshpoetry.co.uk
www.publishandprint.co.uk

Printed in Great Britain
by Amazon